MORE ADVANCE PRAISE FOR
PHYSICIAN, PROTECT THYSELF

"Written by a wise and experienced malpractice defense attorney, Physician, Protect Thyself *is a practical guide for all physicians that clearly explains the basic strategies to prevent malpractice claims. Physicians who follow its sound advice not only will reduce malpractice claims but also will improve the quality of their medical care."*
—James L. Bernat, M.D., Director,
Program in Clinical Ethics
Dartmouth-Hitchcock Medical Center
Professor of Medicine,
Dartmouth Medical School

"Alan G. Williams's book contains a wealth of useful information for medical students, residents and physicians in practice. Following these suggestions will likely both improve the quality of care delivered and reduce the number of malpractice suits."
—Kevin Volpp, M.D., Ph.D., Staff Physician,
Philadelphia VA Medical Center
Assistant Professor of Medicine and Health
Care Systems, University of Pennsylvania
School of Medicine and the Wharton School

*"*Physician, Protect Thyself *is based on years of practical experience by a skilled defense lawyer. It provides a balanced view of malpractice claims and presents a proactive approach for avoiding getting sued. This will be very valuable reading for physicians and physicians-in-training."*
—Antonio M. Grotto, Jr., M.D., D. Phil.
The Stephen and Susan Weiss Dean
Joan and Sanford I. Weill Medical College
Cornell University

"This is a terrific book. It is complete and concise. It should be incorporated into curricula for students, residents and fellows."
— Richard D. Krugman, M.D.
Dean, School of Medicine
University of Colorado

"This outstanding book is filled with practical advice and illuminating real-world vignettes from a leading defense attorney. It belongs in the hands of every physician facing malpractice litigation or, better yet, interested in preventing it."
— Richard E. Anderson, M.D.
Chairman and CEO, The Doctors Company

"Finally, someone has written a simple, concise manual to assist physicians in preventing medical malpractice claims."
— The Florida Medical Association

"A concise, readable and very informative resource for all physicians."
— Adriane Fugh-Berman, M.D., Professor,
Department of Physiology and Biophysics
Georgetown University

"I'm so glad I read Mr. Williams's book while still in my residency. A short, easy read, Physician, Protect Thyself is nonetheless filled with studies and statistics from the medical literature as well as essential practice tips, case examples and practical advice from an attorney whose primary legal practice is defending us when we're sued. I recommend it to every medical student, resident, attending and practicing physician."
— Christopher J. LeCroy, M.D.
Surgical Resident, University of
Alabama-Birmingham School of Medicine

> *Medicine: The only profession that labors incessantly to destroy the reason for its own existence.*
> **—James Bryce**

PHYSICIAN, PROTECT THYSELF

7 Simple Ways NOT to Get Sued for Medical Malpractice

Alan G. Williams, J.D.

Margol Publishing

Physician, Protect Thyself
7 Simple Ways NOT to Get Sued for Medical Malpractice
by Alan G. Williams, J.D.

Published by:
Margol Publishing
Denver, Colorado

ISBN, print ed.   0-9788356-9-7

Printed in the United States of America

Library of Congress Cataloging-in-Publication Data

Library of Congress Control Number: 2006938311

Williams, Alan G., 1965—
Physician, protect thyself / Alan G. Williams.
        p. cm.
Includes biographical references (p.) and index.
ISBN 0-9788356-9-7
1. Physicians—Malpractice—United States.
2. Healthcare/Medical—United States
3. Insurance, Physician's liability—United States. I. Title.
4. Actions and defenses—United States.

Contents

Note to the Reader

For clarity, in this first edition of *Physician, Protect Thyself* the masculine pronoun is utilized to signify health care providers and attorneys, while the feminine pronoun is utilized to signify patients and plaintiffs. The second edition of the book—scheduled for publication in January 2009—will alternate these masculine and feminine designations.

The *Real World Suggestions* at the end of each chapter, and the other suggestions in this book, are recommendations from the legal perspective; as the health care provider, you are in the best position to determine if—based on medical considerations and your professional judgment—some of these suggestions are contraindicated or otherwise inappropriate or inapplicable for your particular medical practice.

Unfortunately, there is not enough room in one book to include everything that every health care provider should know about medical malpractice and the prevention of claims, especially considering medical malpractice law is constantly changing, evolving, and being revised. Consequently, the author and publisher have prepared supplemental materials that are referenced in relevant places throughout this book. You may not want or need these supplements at present, but when you do they are listed in this book's Appendices. The author and publisher pledge to make every effort to update and maintain as current the supplemental materials, as well as this book, through revisions and subsequent editions.

About the Author

Alan G. Williams has been defending physicians, health care providers, hospitals, medical schools and health care facilities his entire legal career. A graduate of Princeton University and the Florida State University College of Law (*High Honors, Order of the Barristers*), he has taught, lectured and spoken to physicians, health care providers, medical students, insurance industry professionals, law students and defense attorneys across the country and serves as an adjunct professor at the Florida State University College of Law teaching medical malpractice law.

Disclaimer

Every effort has been made to assure the accuracy of the information contained in this book; however, the information is current only up to the printing date. This book is sold with the understanding that neither the author nor the publisher is engaged in the rendering of legal services and that no attorney-client relationship—or any other type of professional relationship—has been or will be formed. If legal advice/services are required or desired, it is the sole responsibility of the reader to retain an attorney. Neither author nor publisher is responsible for any errors or omissions or for any consequences from the application of the information presented in this book pertaining to matters of law or medicine and make no warranty, express or implied, with respect to the contents in this publication. The reader is specifically cautioned that medical malpractice laws differ from state to state, and that the only means by which to obtain competent legal advice is by speaking with and/or hiring an attorney licensed to practice law in that particular state.

Dedication

To the teachers, who make everything possible; we're all where we are today because someone showed us the way here. A special thank you goes to Vince Doidge, Sister Margaret Frederick, Annette Massicotte, Coach Pedro Peña, Coach Pete Carril, Professor Nat Stern, Professor Charles Ehrhardt, Professor Rob Atkinson, Henry Burnett and Dan Beasley; along with my family, they truly lit the way.

When surveyed regarding the most important problems facing health care providers today, one third of responding physicians cited medical malpractice lawsuits and insurance; five percent cited medical mistakes or injuries.

Foreword

When the author approached me about writing the Foreword for this book, I initially hesitated, questioning what of significance I might offer on the subject of reducing medical malpractice claims. But my hesitation was only momentary because, as I considered it, I realized every physician has at least something to add to this, at times, quite personal topic; and, I believe my fourteen years as Dean of the University of Miami School of Medicine responsible for the final client decisions regarding medical malpractice claims filed against the School of Medicine for care rendered in one of the nation's largest medical centers provides me more medical-legal experience than most. Malpractice claims and malpractice law certainly have changed dramatically over the course of my forty-five-year professional career, and in my former position as Dean I dealt with every kind of claim imaginable, in virtually every medical specialty and practice area. However, throughout the years and over the course of many cases, one thing has remained unwaveringly constant—health care providers themselves have always had the ability to reduce and prevent malpractice claims.

The political debate may rage on regarding malpractice lawsuits and their effects on society, the practice of medicine, physicians' careers and lives. Professional organizations, industry groups, lobbying firms and politicians may attempt to influence and pass legislation to curb what is termed "the medical malpractice crisis." New laws may limit the amount of damages injured patients can recover, restrict patients' ability to file claims, reduce the fee plaintiffs lawyers take from an award. Yet, despite all these measures, insurance industry executives testify that medical malpractice insurance premiums would not be reduced by any of the above-mentioned strategies. As physicians, we're then left wondering what we can do to address the problem.

Countless studies and statistics detail the number of frivolous lawsuits filed, the millions of dollars awarded plaintiffs for questionable claims. We read about physicians relocating to flee exorbitant malpractice insurance premiums, or retiring all together. The television news broadcasts scenes of doctors on strike to protest rising malpractice insurance premiums, or walk-outs at hospitals, emergency rooms and trauma centers. We all know the world we live in and, although we might not like it, we can't control it. But there are aspects of our practice we can control, proactive steps we all can take to improve our situations, recommendations we can heed to change the statistics, the studies, the news reports.

The University of Miami School of Medicine, like many large hospitals and medical centers, is primarily self-insured, so my medical-legal experiences do not come from malpractice insurers or claims adjusters, but from defense attorneys and plaintiffs lawyers, from risk managers and in-house investigators, from physicians and plaintiff patients. As the client, I dealt directly with the principles in malpractice cases, personally gave hundreds of depositions in my capacity as chief administrative officer, testified in courtrooms on multiple occasions, and I must confess that, in general, my experiences with malpractice claims and the American legal system have left me with a healthy respect for the manner in which claims are resolved. As they say, it might not be a perfect legal system, but I have yet to find one better.

We physicians often find ourselves criticizing the legal system, harping about the trial lawyers who sue us, complaining about runaway juries breaking the bank for malingering ex-patients, but based on my experiences I have nothing but respect for a legal system that allows someone who truly believes she was injured to have her day in court, and I can't recall one plaintiff I would have begrudged that opportunity. Physicians naturally may be fearful of lawsuits, of having their care publicly criticized, of facing reprimand or suspension, but the possibility of malpractice lawsuits is attenuate to every medical practice, and the best way to deal with that fear is to arm yourself with the knowledge that will enable you to prevent the claims you can.

We are all taught the Ten Commandments in medical school; we all know the rules, the steps to take, the procedures to follow. But it's when we relax those rules, stray a bit from those commandments, start cutting those corners, that the plaintiffs lawyers appear on the scene. Physicians may want to complain about frivolous lawsuits, but the vast majority of malpractice claims I have overseen throughout my career might never have happened if that health care provider had just followed the procedures, heeded the commandments, not relaxed the rules. It may seem minor, but simply timing your notes, reading an intake questionnaire, thoroughly writing out patient instructions, documenting a complete and thorough physical examination—any of these could be the difference between no claim being filed against you or five years of litigation followed by a massive jury award rendered against you. You may not be able to control every aspect of whether you are sued, but you certainly should strive to control those you can.

I, of course, firmly believe that improving patient care is the number one step we as physicians can take to reduce the chances of having a malpractice claim filed against us, but this book does not provide medical recommendations in an attempt to reduce claims. We already have sufficient medical resources available that delineate all the ways in which to improve the care we render. As a defense attorney, the author of this book seeks to reduce claims through recommendations offered from the legal standpoint. My years at the University, however, have taught me that reducing claims from a legal standpoint invariably leads to improved patient care. It may seem circular, but we as physicians should not only strive medically to improve patient care but to reduce claims by following recommendations made from the legal standpoint, and in a wonderful yet productive irony, these legal recommendations in and of themselves may also lead to improved patient care.

The author is one of the many defense attorneys I worked with over the course of my long career, and I recall not only his joining our defense firm as a young lawyer many years ago, but his first medical malpractice trial for us, as well as his last (both defense verdicts). For years we in academic medicine have sought a reference manual with which we can teach medical students, residents and young physicians how best to reduce the chances of being sued for malpractice, how to improve patient care from the legal standpoint. I am proud to say this book succinctly yet clearly outlines the ways in which you yourself can reduce and prevent claims. Having worked with the author for years in the defense of malpractice claims, I know from personal experience that following this book's recommendations will definitely result in the reduction of medical malpractice claims. And that is a goal for which we all should be striving, if not for our patients' sakes, then for our own.

Bernard J. Fogel, M.D., *Dean Emeritus*,
Leonard M. Miller School of Medicine at
the University of Miami

Jackson Memorial Medical Center—the primary teaching hospital affiliated with the University of Miami School of Medicine—is the largest public hospital, and third busiest medical center, in the country.

A

The ABCs of a
Medical Malpractice Claim
Introduction

*We have not lost faith, but we have transferred it
from God to the medical profession.*
—George Bernard Shaw

Nothing can help you if you consistently practice medicine below the accepted standard of care; you will eventually be sued for malpractice and find yourself on the losing end of a jury verdict or settlement. No one, or nothing written in any book, has to tell you to practice medicine to the best of your abilities, to utilize the available technology, resources and your own training and experience to provide optimal patient care. This book assumes you attempt your best every day, that you do everything within your power to be a competent, professional health care provider who renders appropriate medical care.

But, everyone makes mistakes; in every profession there are excellent practitioners who, even just once in their careers, miss something. Every single person in every single occupation makes honest mistakes, usually every single day. But when that teacher, or waiter, or garbage collector, or lawyer makes a mistake, it can typically be rectified quite easily. In the medical profession, however, when a health care provider makes a mistake, patients can be seriously injured or die. This is, of course, what may lead a patient or patient's family to file a medical malpractice claim.

This book seeks to help you prevent being sued for medical malpractice in cases where you provided medical care that, at a minimum, meets the accepted standard; it may also assist you in precluding a medical malpractice claim in cases where, for some reason, you may not have provided the appropriate level of care. Additionally, this book outlines specific procedural and proactive steps to help reduce your chances of having a medical malpractice claim filed against you, steps that may also improve your medical practice and the quality of care you provide.

You certainly can skip forward to the seven numbered chapters and read about how to avoid and prevent medical malpractice claims, but it first may assist you to know what a medical malpractice claim really is, why a patient might file one, how a medical malpractice claim progresses, and what can happen to resolve a claim once a patient does file one. In your daily medical practice you may read about and hear terms such as *claims, lawsuits, plaintiffs lawyers* or *trial lawyers, interrogatories, expert witnesses, jury awards, settlements, cross-examination, depositions, trials* and *verdicts*. But what do these terms really mean? Where do you go if you have a question about something you did, or witnessed someone else do? Who is on *your* side? The three introductory chapters explain the ins and outs of medical malpractice claims, providing you a concise yet thorough outline of the medical-legal process.

> **Real World Numbers:** *Prior to 1960, only one in seven physicians was sued for medical malpractice throughout his entire career; currently, one in seven physicians is sued for medical malpractice every year. Other studies approximate as many as 25% of all physicians are sued each year, and as many as 65% of all physicians will be sued sometime during their careers.*

By way of author introduction, I am a medical malpractice defense attorney and have been my entire legal career. I have defended physicians, residents, interns, medical students, medical schools, nurses, physician assistants, psychologists, dentists, podiatrists, phlebotomists, laboratory and radiologic technicians, nursing students, hospitals, hospital administrators, medical facilities, health care offices and malpractice insurance companies. I have taught, lectured and spoken to physicians, health care providers, medical students, insurance industry professionals, law students and other defense attorneys across the country. I have never once represented a patient or patient's family against a health care provider. My uncle and cousin are both physicians, another cousin a trauma nurse, and my sister-in-law a physician assistant; I could never attend another family function if I broke ranks, went over to *the dark side*, and began suing health care providers on behalf of patients.

Although I have a doctorate, I am not a medical doctor and would never presume to be qualified to advise a health care provider how to improve his practice from the medical perspective; however, I have been told too many times by too many physicians that improving one's medical practice from the legal perspective invariably leads to improved patient care from the medical perspective. It is with this caveat that all recommendations in this book are offered.

These first three chapters—Chapter A, Chapter B and Chapter C—comprise the ABCs of a medical malpractice claim, detailing what exactly a medical malpractice claim is, how you may find yourself involved in one, why patients file medical malpractice claims, and a brief outline of the basics of a medical malpractice trial. The seven subsequent chapters provide simple yet effective ways you can help protect yourself from a medical malpractice claim ever being filed against you. However, despite my status as a lawyer, this book is not intended as legal advice. Every state and jurisdiction is different, every circumstance and case unique. No one can provide you thorough, competent legal advice via a book or manual; the only way you can receive such advice is by speaking with a medical malpractice defense attorney licensed to practice law in your state, who knows the detailed ins and outs of the medical malpractice laws unique to your jurisdiction. Appendix A lists supplemental materials regarding the medical malpractice laws of your particular state, and Appendix D provides resources to assist in locating a defense attorney within your state who can answer specific questions you may have; but, as the following chapters explain, your employer, medical facility or malpractice insurance carrier most likely has defense attorneys available to help you should the need arise. This book seeks to assist you prevent a medical malpractice claim before it starts; once you've been sued, this book may provide you with useful information, but only a defense attorney can appropriately represent you and defend legally the medical care you rendered.

In the event you are sued for medical malpractice, it is imperative you remember it is not the end of the world. Being sued certainly is a stressful, difficult situation, but you cannot let it ruin your life. I have seen too many physicians become obsessed with a pending medical malpractice lawsuit, to the point it affects their medical practice, personal life, marriage, etc. If I could offer only one recommendation you remember after reading this book, it is that if you are sued, let your defense attorney do his job; don't allow a lawsuit to negatively impact what is truly important in your life. We're all human (even lawyers), and at the end of the day most people simply want to be home, safe, at peace. This book seeks, in some small way, to assist health care providers in pursuit of that goal.

B

The ABCs of a Medical Malpractice Claim
Why Patients Sue

It is not a case we are treating; it is a living, palpitating, alas, too often suffering fellow creature.
—John Brown

Most patients do not want to sue you. Despite what you hear on television or read in newspapers or medical journals, only a small fraction of patients ever consider suing their health care providers. In fact, a Harvard study reported that less than three percent (<3%) of hospitalized patients who suffered injuries or death attributable to medical negligence actually filed medical malpractice claims. Most people respect and admire health care providers immensely, and the idea that patients as a whole are a greedy, litigious lot hell-bent on filing a medical malpractice claim at the mere hint of substandard care could not be farther from the truth. But what does transform a patient into a medical malpractice plaintiff may surprise you, and knowing such can assist you in preventing your patients from ever becoming plaintiffs.

Real World Vocabulary

Medical Malpractice or **Medical Negligence** *is the practice of medicine below what is the accepted minimum standard of care within a given community, jurisdiction or practice area. When you practice medicine below the minimum standard of care you have committed medical negligence and may be found liable for such in a civil court of law. Health care providers themselves set the minimum standard of care in a community via their own routines, protocols and practice, but it is the expert witness who defines the standard of care in a medical malpractice lawsuit by offering testimony regarding the minimum standard of care that must be practiced. The term "malpractice" is derived from Sir William Blackstone's 1765-1767 legal treatise* Commentaries on the Laws of England, *which utilized the term "mala praxis," defined as injuries caused by the neglect or unskilled management by a physician that breaks the patient's trust.*

A **Medical Malpractice Claim** *is the formal, procedural allegation that a health care provider has committed medical negligence. In some states a claim is filed with a review board or in a preliminary procedure prior to an actual lawsuit being filed within the civil court system.*

Medical Malpractice Lawsuit *refers to a medical malpractice claim that has progressed to the point an actual lawsuit alleging medical negligence has been filed in the civil court system. Even after a lawsuit is filed the term "claim" is still oftentimes utilized. In this book, "claim" refers only to those proceedings prior to an actual legal case being filed in the civil court system, and "lawsuit" refers only to a case filed in the civil court system.*

A **Complaint** *is the legal term for a lawsuit that has been filed; the Complaint is the actual commencement of the lawsuit within the civil court system. When a health care* provider is sued for medical negligence, he receives a copy of the Complaint, which is a written document created by the plaintiffs lawyer that lays out the grounds for the lawsuit, including the factual allegations, alleged negligence and alleged injuries resulting from the alleged negligence. The defense attorney representing the health care provider responds to the Complaint by filing an **Answer** (or **Response**), the formal, written defense to the allegations raised in the Complaint. The Complaint and Answer are actual pieces of paper filed with the court.

A **Plaintiff** (or occasionally **Petitioner** or **Claimant**) is the person making the allegation of medical negligence who actually brings the claim or lawsuit. It is either the patient or, if the patient is deceased, mentally incompetent or a minor, the patient's family or representative.

A **Plaintiffs Lawyer** is the attorney representing the plaintiff and filing the claim or lawsuit on her behalf. The media often refer to plaintiffs lawyers as **Trial Lawyers**, a misnomer, as any attorney who engages in litigation is a trial lawyer; as a defense attorney who litigates in the courtroom on behalf of health care providers, I am a trial lawyer.

Defendant (or occasionally **Respondent**) is the individual health care provider or corporate entity (i.e., hospital, medical facility, insurer, medical school, etc.) accused of committing medical negligence who is then forced to defend himself/itself.

A **Defense Attorney** is a lawyer who defends claims and lawsuits, representing the defendant health care provider.

An **Expert Witness** is a health care provider (typically within the same field or specialty as the health care provider accused of medical negligence) hired by either the plaintiffs lawyer or the defense attorney to review the medical records and offer an opinion regarding the medical care rendered by the defendant health care provider, including defining the standard of care. An expert witness may also testify regarding the cause and/or extent of injuries suffered by the plaintiff. In order to present a viable medical malpractice claim, the plaintiffs lawyer must almost always produce an expert witness willing to testify that the defendant health care provider did indeed commit medical negligence.

Interrogatories are written questions lawyers exchange regarding the lawsuit's allegations. The defense attorney will contact the defendant health care provider to assist in responding to the interrogatories posed by the plaintiffs lawyer. **Requests for Production** are written requests lawyers make to each other, asking the other side to provide copies of certain things (e.g., the defense attorney requests copies of the plaintiff's tax returns to show the plaintiff is still employed and making the same amount of money she did prior to the alleged medical negligence; the plaintiffs lawyer requests copies of incident reports regarding surgeries similar to the one involved in the lawsuit). **Requests for Admissions** are written questions asking a party to formally admit or deny some fact (e.g., "Admit or deny it is a violation of the applicable standard of care not to order a CT scan when a patient suffers head trauma resulting in loss of consciousness and subsequently complains of dizziness, nausea, vomiting and frequent headaches.").

A **Deposition** is a pre-trial legal proceeding wherein attorneys ask a witness questions under oath, a permanent, written transcript of which is created. Depositions are typically held in a law firm's conference room, or a conference room in a hospital or office building, and customarily the only persons present are the plaintiffs lawyer and defense attorney, a court reporter (typing everything said into a stenographer's machine) and the testifying witness; no judge or jury is present. The testimony witnesses give during depositions shapes the progress of the lawsuit and indicates to attorneys whether the case should be settled, proceed to trial, or perhaps even dismissed by the judge. Medical malpractice lawsuits are oftentimes effectively won or lost during depositions, usually during the defendant health care provider's deposition or, occasionally, during the plaintiff's.

Cross-examination occurs when an attorney questions a witness—either during deposition or trial—who is most likely adverse to that attorney's client; the plaintiffs lawyer conducts the cross-examination of the defendant health care provider, the defense attorney conducts the cross-examination of the plaintiff. For the defendant health care provider, deposition cross-examination is typically the most stressful (yet most important) pre-trial aspect of a medical malpractice lawsuit. A competent defense attorney will ensure the health care provider is adequately prepared for deposition and cross-examination, frequently practicing with the health care provider prior to any such testimony.

Summary Judgment is a legal ruling that in essence signifies the end of a lawsuit prior to it ever reaching trial. Oftentimes a defense attorney will file legal documents with the court requesting the judge end the case on legal grounds, precluding the case from proceeding to trial and effectively concluding the lawsuit with no monies paid to the plaintiffs. The granting of summary judgment in favor of a defendant health care provider is rare but by far the best possible result because the lawsuit concludes immediately (in the absence of an appeal to a higher court). The granting of a **Motion to Dismiss** may not signify a permanent conclusion to the lawsuit (although it may), but such a ruling is a similar victory for the defendant health care provider.

A **Jury Verdict** is the decision rendered by a jury in a lawsuit that has progressed all the way through trial. In a medical malpractice case, a jury verdict is either "no liability," which means the defendant health care provider did not commit medical negligence legally responsible for a patient's injury, or "liable," which means the defendant health care provider is held legally responsible for a patient's injury resulting from medical negligence. A jury verdict of "liable" also results in a **Jury Award**, the rendering of a dollar figure for damages against the defendant health care provider to be paid to the plaintiff.

Settlement refers to concluding a medical malpractice claim or lawsuit by mutual agreement of the parties, with the defendant health care provider usually paying monies in exchange for the plaintiff voluntarily dismissing the claim or lawsuit. Settlement can occur anytime after the adverse medical incident, all the way through the actual trial.

Individual health care providers typically loathe settlements, but insurers, hospitals, medical facilities, health care systems and medical schools utilize settlements as a way to decrease monetary exposure in cases where an adverse jury verdict may result in a massive jury award and/or intense negative publicity. A plaintiffs lawyer oftentimes realizes what once appeared a sure-fire trial victory accompanied by a windfall jury award now looks like a possible loser, and therefore accepts a token settlement, which is offered by the defendant health care provider merely to dismiss the case and forego the costs of trial and the accompanying publicity.

It is important to note that a medical malpractice lawsuit is a civil—not criminal—proceeding. You cannot be sent to jail if you are found "liable" (as opposed to "guilty") of medical negligence. The American civil justice system deals almost exclusively with money and the exchange of money as a means to address what has been ruled unjust by a judge or jury. A claim of medical negligence does not seek to incarcerate you or take away your liberty—the only thing that may be taken is money (which typically is paid by your malpractice insurer or employer, unless you are uninsured). Although, as the following paragraphs explain, oftentimes plaintiffs don't really want money; they may simply want acknowledgment of a wrong, recognition of an injury, or just an apology. But the only thing a civil court in the American justice system can award a plaintiff is money.

> ***Real World Numbers:*** *Some studies approximate only 17% of medical malpractice claims actually involve injury caused by negligent medical treatment.*

Numerous studies have attempted to determine why patients file medical malpractice claims against their health care providers, the results of which consistently point to four general motivations:

- they felt their health care provider deserted them

- they felt their views and concerns were not valued by their health care provider

- they felt information was not effectively relayed to them by their health care provider

- they felt their health care provider failed to understand their perspective

Additionally, patients and their families also cite another factor when deciding whether to initiate a medical malpractice claim: the health care provider's insensitive handling/poor communication following the original complication or adverse incident, and the suspicion that the health care provider or medical facility was attempting to cover something up. This factor may be the most important, as it reveals that, even after committing medical negligence resulting in injury to a patient, a health care provider may in fact preclude a medical malpractice claim simply by frank, open, effective communication; even after you've committed malpractice, you still have the ability to prevent a medical malpractice claim by the manner in which you handle subsequent communications and events. And, as most claims begin with some kind of complication that, in and of itself, is not malpractice, it is how you manage that complication that typically is the difference whether a medical malpractice claim is eventually filed.

Real World Numbers: *A comprehensive study published in the* Archives of Internal Medicine, *focused solely on parents whose children suffered permanent injuries or death due to alleged adverse medical incidents, found that 24% filed a medical malpractice claim in part because they believed the health care providers were trying to hide something or cover something up, and 20% filed a claim in part because they wanted more information regarding what happened to their children. The parents in the study expressed extreme dissatisfaction with* physician-patient communication; 48% believed the physician attempted to mislead them, 32% believed the physician refused to speak openly about the incident, and 13% believed the physician would not listen to them.

A separate study conducted by researchers at MIT and the University of Michigan found that patients filed medical malpractice claims in large part merely to determine if the health care provider was negligent, and once the claim or lawsuit revealed that appropriate care was in fact provided, the plaintiff tended to drop the case. A Harvard study published in 2006 in the New England Journal of Medicine reached a similar conclusion.

The studies regarding why patients file medical malpractice claims appear to show that when a patient feels valued, that her opinion matters and that she is receiving open, active communication, she is far less likely to contact a plaintiffs lawyer regarding initiating a claim. Chapter 1 specifically addresses these patient concerns as a means to help prevent a potential medical malpractice claim being filed against you; it is imperative to both your medical practice and career that you remain cognizant of the primary reasons patients file medical malpractice claims. Those who forget history are doomed to repeat it.

C

The ABCs of a
Medical Malpractice Claim
The Claim and Subsequent Lawsuit

The only equipment lack in the modern hospital?
Somebody to meet you at the entrance with a
handshake.
—Martin H. Fischer

Your patient, for whatever reason, has made the decision to contact a plaintiffs lawyer regarding a possible medical malpractice claim. Whether or not a claim is actually filed against you, or if you are sued for medical malpractice, is now beyond your control. The plaintiffs lawyer—and his team of medical investigators and expert witnesses—has become the sole arbiter whether any legal action is initiated against you. A judge or jury may ultimately decide your fate, but until that time it is the plaintiffs lawyer who controls what happens regarding the potential medical malpractice claim.

Medical Malpractice, Legally: *For a patient to have a legally cognizable claim for medical malpractice, four requirements must first exist:*

- *a legal duty (such as the legal duty a health care provider has to appropriately treat a patient)*

- *breach of that legal duty (such as the health care provider not rendering appropriate medical care)*

- *an injury (such as the patient dying, or losing a limb, or becoming even more infirm than when she originally presented to the health care provider)*

- *breach of the legal duty actually causing the injury (such as a physician prescribing a medication that is contraindicated, resulting in the patient's death, or a physician amputating the wrong limb)*

In general, the patient presents herself at the plaintiffs lawyer's office, producing her medical records and relating the events surrounding the adverse medical incident. The plaintiffs lawyer asks questions and discusses the patient's present medical condition/prognosis and then gives the medical records to a medical investigator (usually a former nurse). If the plaintiffs lawyer and medical investigator—in consultation subsequent to a review of the medical records—believe there may be grounds for a medical malpractice claim, the plaintiffs lawyer typically forwards the medical records to an expert witness for review. If, after reviewing the medical records, the expert witness believes no medical negligence in fact occurred (and the plaintiffs lawyer cannot find another expert witness willing to testify that medical negligence did occur), then no claim for medical malpractice is filed and the incident is simply dropped. If, however, the expert witness does believe a health care provider may have rendered substandard medical care resulting in injury to the patient, the plaintiffs lawyer then proceeds with a claim.

Each state prescribes its own legal requirements for patients desiring to commence a medical malpractice claim, and the plaintiffs lawyer would initiate a formal claim by complying with those requirements (e.g., contacting the state medical board, or filing documents and medical records with a medical review panel, or forwarding a claim to the defendant health care provider, or filing a preliminary allegation with the court, etc.). When the state's requirements are met, the plaintiffs lawyer may then file a formal medical malpractice lawsuit in the state civil court system (although there are various opportunities for the claim never to proceed to the point a lawsuit is filed, such as a medical review panel or court dismissing the claim for lack of sufficient evidence of negligence, the claim reaching monetary settlement, etc.).

The plaintiffs lawyer files the Complaint in the civil court system, and then the defense attorney files the health care provider's Answer. Prior to the commencement of the lawsuit, you most likely will have dealt with the claim in some way, at a minimum being made aware of it by the plaintiffs lawyer, a defense attorney, or your malpractice insurer or medical facility. [If you receive a demand letter or any other type of communication from a patient's lawyer, do not attempt to contact that lawyer or the patient, or to conduct any investigation or inquiry, without first discussing the incident with your legal representative or a medical administrator.] The filing of a lawsuit should then not surprise you, but if it does, the first thing you should do is contact your supervisor, administrator, malpractice insurer or defense attorney. A multitude of time requirements exist in the legal system, and there is a finite period in which to respond to a Complaint. If you do receive a Complaint (typically from a process server, or perhaps even from a sheriff's deputy), alert someone immediately.

Once your defense attorney contacts you—which typically occurs after the plaintiffs lawyer initiates the claim but may not occur until the Complaint is filed—he will instruct you what to do. The lawsuit will then progress with the exchange of interrogatories and requests for production between the plaintiffs lawyer and your defense attorney. Eventually your deposition will be taken, as well as the depositions of the plaintiff, fact witnesses and expert witnesses. The court may conduct hearings during this discovery phase of the lawsuit, attempting to resolve legal disagreements between the attorneys (e.g., the plaintiffs lawyer requests copies of medical records of other patients undergoing the same type of surgery to see if their bleeding times were checked every fifteen minutes instead of the thirty minutes the plaintiff's bleeding times were checked, but the defense attorney objects to producing the medical records on the grounds of patient privacy; or, the plaintiffs lawyer fights the defense attorney's request to question the plaintiff's twelve-year-old son to determine if the plaintiff was in fact an alcoholic prior to the alleged negligence as opposed to the alcoholism being caused by injuries resulting from the alleged medical negligence, as the plaintiff claims). There may be large gaps of inactivity during a medical malpractice lawsuit, and even if action and/or progress is occurring, you may not hear anything for weeks or months. The lawsuit, however, is slowly progressing, despite your belief it is stagnant.

Real World Numbers: *A typical medical malpractice lawsuit lasts approximately four and a half years, from the initial filing of the Complaint until final resolution.*

At any time subsequent to the adverse medical incident that gave rise to the medical malpractice claim or lawsuit, a settlement may be entered into between the plaintiff and defendant health care provider, effectively concluding the claim or lawsuit. However, you may not have a choice whether the case against you settles, despite the fact it is your medical care being criticized. Although some medical malpractice insurance policies contain "consent" provisions—meaning you would have to agree to and give your consent to any settlement before your malpractice insurer could settle the case on your behalf—your malpractice policy may not (some states outlaw consent provisions as against public policy). If you are employed by a hospital, medical facility or health care system, you may have little or no control whether the case against you is settled.

Lawsuits settle for various reasons, ranging from the fear of negative publicity or a massive jury award to the plaintiffs lawyer realizing he simply doesn't have as strong a case as he thought and your malpractice insurer merely pays nuisance value to save the costs of further defending the lawsuit. These are the realities of the medical-legal system, but if you truly desire the ultimate veto power over a proposed settlement you should contact your medical malpractice insurance carrier. As a defense attorney, I firmly believe in the utility and necessity of settlements; if you have ever been sued for medical malpractice, you most likely feel the same, as a claim/lawsuit that might have taken years to resolve only to result in a negative outcome at trial is instead quickly over, with a minimum of time, stress and effort expended by the defendant health care provider. Until you've been subjected to rigorous cross-examination, both during your deposition and at trial, you cannot know how beneficial avoiding those experiences can be. We'd all like to defend our names and reputations to the bitter end, but without settlements, a medical malpractice case could very well lead to a bitter end indeed.

Defense attorneys, however, do not make the decision whether to settle a case; that is up to the client— the insurer, the hospital, the health care system, the medical facility, the health care provider. Nothing gives a defense attorney more satisfaction than seeing a case all the way through trial and obtaining a jury verdict of "no liability." It is our World Series, our Super Bowl, our March Madness all rolled into one, and my greatest thrill as an attorney comes when I can hug a defendant health care provider I've gotten to know quite well over the few years of working together defending a case and say, "it's over; you won." Other than obtaining a summary judgment in favor of the defendant health care provider or a complete dismissal of the case in the early stages, nothing beats going to trial and winning. Your defense attorney wants to fight for you; sometimes, however, discretion is the better part of valor and settlement the most prudent option.

Should the lawsuit against you not resolve or settle, it will proceed to trial (although most medical malpractice lawsuits do settle or resolve prior to trial). Depending on the care involved, the number of defendants and the type of injuries suffered, a medical malpractice trial may last anywhere from a few days to, in rare instances, a few months. Trials can be long, exhausting and oftentimes boring, but your defense attorney will explain everything to you, from what to wear all the way through how to act while you're merely sitting at defense table. It is imperative you know that the jury sees everything, that they are constantly watching you, as you are the reason they are there. Do not do anything or act in any way that will negatively impact the jury's impression of you, no matter how frustrated you are to be there or how ludicrous you find the proceedings.

Real World Example: *A physician was one of two defendants in a medical malpractice trial merely because he was tangentially involved in the plaintiff's care and his office was located in a jurisdiction the plaintiffs lawyer believed favorable to his client. Throughout the trial the physician visibly acted as if he loathed being present—he stared at the ceiling, read magazines, made personal cellular phones calls when the jury was still present in the courtroom and acted disdainfully on the witness stand— as if he were too important to waste his time sitting there defending his care. Despite his medical care not being the primary target of the plaintiff's lawsuit and the allegations of negligence against him suspicious at best, the jury found him negligent and partially liable for the plaintiff's injuries.*

A trial begins with jury selection, where the attorneys and judge question potential jurors in an effort to determine if they can be fair and impartial (in fact, each attorney attempts to select jurors he believes will be favorable to his client). Subsequent to selection of a jury, the plaintiffs lawyer presents an opening statement, describing what happened to the plaintiff and outlining the evidence he will present in support of his assertion the health care provider committed medical negligence resulting in injury to the plaintiff. He will also describe the current medical condition of the plaintiff, especially where severe, permanent injuries were suffered. The defense attorney will then give his opening statement, introducing the defendant health care provider in an attempt to humanize and personalize him for the jury, and outlining the evidence that shows no medical negligence occurred.

The plaintiffs lawyer then presents his case, typically calling an expert witness to testify why what happened was in fact medical negligence, and what injuries the plaintiff suffered because of the negligence. Depending on the type of case and the number of defendants, the plaintiffs lawyer may present numerous expert witnesses. Fact witnesses may then be called (typically the plaintiff's friends or family members), testifying as to what injuries the plaintiff now has or, occasionally, what the witness heard or saw at the time of the incident. Then the plaintiff herself will testify, telling her story. [The testimony of the plaintiff and testimony of the defendant health care provider are the two most important aspects of a medical malpractice trial, and are typically where the trial is won or lost.] The plaintiffs lawyer may then present some type of testimony or evidence regarding what dollar amount he believes will compensate the plaintiff for her injuries. The defense attorney cross-examines each of the plaintiff's witnesses immediately after that witness testifies on behalf of the plaintiff. The plaintiffs lawyer may even call the defendant health care provider to testify during the plaintiff's case, cross-examining him in an attempt to elicit responses most helpful to the plaintiff. The defense attorney would then also question the defendant health care provider to provide testimony helpful to the defense. After calling his witnesses and presenting all his evidence, the plaintiffs lawyer then rests his case.

The defense attorney typically will then ask the judge—via a *Motion for Directed Verdict*—to end the trial/lawsuit by entering a verdict in favor of the defendant health care provider on the grounds the plaintiffs lawyer failed to meet the burden of proof. To prevail in a civil court proceeding, the plaintiff must prove her case by a preponderance of the evidence (a much lower standard of proof than the "beyond a reasonable doubt" standard of proof in a criminal trial, which is sometimes described as a 99% certainty); a preponderance of the evidence standard of proof is oftentimes described as tipping the scales of justice ever so slightly in the plaintiff's favor, a 51% certainty. [You may remember the two O.J. Simpson trials, where Simpson was found not guilty of murder in the criminal trial because the case was not proven beyond a reasonable doubt but was found liable in the wrongful death civil action because the case was proven by a preponderance of the evidence.] The judge usually denies the defense attorney's Motion for Directed Verdict—although occasionally such a motion succeeds, effectively ending the case—and then the defense attorney proceeds with presenting the defense case.

Real World Numbers: *A study published in the* New England Journal of Medicine *found that, in medical malpractice claims lacking merit, one in four resulted in some form of compensation paid to the plaintiff, whether through jury award, settlement or some other means.*

The defense attorney calls his expert witnesses to testify why no medical negligence occurred, and why any injuries the plaintiff suffered were not as a result of any alleged negligence. Fact witnesses may also be called to refute the plaintiff's fact witnesses, or to show further evidence helpful to the defense. The defense attorney will then call the defendant health care provider—if the plaintiffs lawyer did not call him during the plaintiff's case—to testify regarding what happened and why, and to explain to the jury in his own words why he did not render negligent medical care. The plaintiffs lawyer cross-examines the defense witnesses immediately after they testify on behalf of the defense. After the defense attorney presents all the witnesses and evidence to show no negligence resulting in injury to the plaintiff occurred, the defense attorney rests his case.

The plaintiffs lawyer then presents his closing argument, summarizing the evidence in a manner most favorable to his client, and the defense attorney does the same. The judge then instructs the jury what specific questions it must answer (e.g., "Was Dr. Smith negligent?"; "If Dr. Smith was negligent, did such negligence result in injury to the plaintiff?"; "If Dr. Smith was negligent resulting in injury to the plaintiff, what amount would adequately compensate the plaintiff for the injuries she suffered due to Dr. Smith's negligence?"). The jury then retires to the jury room to deliberate. Once the jury reaches a verdict it is read in open court and the formal legal decision regarding the case entered. If the defendant health care provider prevails, the plaintiff may appeal and attempt to have a higher court declare the jury's verdict incorrect, arguing there should be a new trial; if the plaintiff prevails, the defense attorney may attempt the same thing on behalf of the defendant health care provider. If no appeal is sought, or any appeal sought denied by a higher court, the case is finally resolved and concluded. If the defendant health care provider has been ordered to pay damages to the plaintiff, monies are transmitted from one party to the other. If the defendant health care provider prevails, he may attempt to seek attorneys fees and costs from the plaintiff (in states where so allowed).

There are numerous texts available that much more fully describe—from soup to nuts, backwards and forwards—a medical malpractice trial; however, if you are sued and/or involved in a medical malpractice trial, your defense attorney should be your first and best resource regarding what a lawsuit or trial entails. This book does not seek to explain medical malpractice lawsuits or trials; this book is designed to help you avoid ever being sued in the first place.

One study found that physicians rated in the bottom third of patient satisfaction surveys had a 110% increased risk of incurring a patient complaint or risk management episode compared to physicians rated in the top third of patient satisfaction surveys.

1

The Real Golden Rule
Your Best Defense

The doctor may also learn more about the illness from the way the patient tells the story than from the story itself.
—James Herrick

Believe it or not, the single most effective tool in preventing medical malpractice claims is "bedside manner." Something that seems so rudimentary—and is more closely related to lessons learned in kindergarten than any course taught in medical school—may very well prevent you from enduring the professional and personal tribulation of being sued for malpractice. In truth, however, it really may be that simple: if your patient does not want to sue you, she won't. Through your own manner and personality, a professional kindness and caring patients immediately recognize, you hold the most important key to averting a medical malpractice claim before it ever starts. If you can prevent that patient from even considering filing a claim against you, she will never contact a lawyer, never ask her friends if they know any malpractice lawyers, never search the internet or the telephone book for law firms willing to take her case.

Once a patient gets over that hump and decides she does indeed want to contact a lawyer, you have zero control whether a claim is filed against you. But, even subsequent to an adverse medical incident, you do have at least some control whether the patient ever gets over that hump, ever decides she wants to explore filing a medical malpractice claim. However, once a patient meets with a medical malpractice plaintiffs lawyer, the possibility of a claim being filed against you rests solely with that plaintiffs lawyer and his expert witness.

Real World Facts: *A study published in the* Journal of the American Medical Association *found that physicians who never had a medical malpractice claim filed against them*

- *laughed and used more humor*
- *asked patients their opinions*
- *encouraged patients to talk and interact*
- *educated patients regarding expectations*
- *spent, on average, over three minutes more with patients during routine visits*

compared with physicians who previously had medical malpractice claims filed against them. Another study concluded that a physician's risk of having a claim filed against him was related to his failures to establish rapport, communicate effectively and fulfill patient expectations. Physicians who had multiple medical malpractice claims filed against them were much more likely to have other complaints lodged against them for not returning phone calls, acting in a rude or disrespectful manner, or refusing to listen to their patients.

In this day and age of managed health ca. HMOs and PPOs, of Medicare and Medicaid, physicians and health care practitioners have so much less time and so many more responsibilities than they did even just a decade ago. Yet that patient waiting on an examining table, or in a surgical suite, or in an emergency room—and those jurors deciding a health care provider's fate in a courtroom years after that patient was actually treated—cares nothing of those realities. That patient may be your fifteenth of the day, but you are her first and only doctor. She wants to be treated with respect, concern and understanding. If you are able to do so, and are able to convey a genuine sense of professional expertise combined with some degree of empathy and human caring, you have greatly decreased the chances of being sued in cases where a patient experiences, or thinks she experiences, an injury caused by medical negligence.

Research indicates that to convince a patient you are actually speaking to her, she must be looking at you approximately 80% of the time and you must be looking at her 95% of the time. It is of course impossible to maintain eye contact or stare into a patient's face throughout the entire patient encounter, but when you are communicating important information or rendering medical instructions you must do all you can to look directly at the patient (not impart vital medical knowledge with your head buried in the chart or interspersed between conversation with another health care provider). Something as seemingly innocuous as sitting down may make a difference, as research indicates patients believe a physician who sits down, versus one who stands, has spent more time with the patient even though time spent with the patient was in actuality exactly the same. [Other studies indicate that when physicians face more than 45 degrees away from their patients, patients tend to have a negative perception of the visit.] When that patient walks out of the examination room or medical facility believing that you care about her, that you took your time, that you treated her with respect and that you communicated with her directly, openly and politely, odds are she will not want to file a medical malpractice claim against you.

Real World Example: Upon referral from her primary care physician, a patient presented to an otolaryngologist complaining of tinnitus accompanied by a slight loss of hearing. The otolaryngologist—who previously had two malpractice claims filed against him, both ultimately dismissed for lack of evidence—performed a complete examination and work-up, along with diagnostic testing, but was unable to determine the cause of her complaints. The complaints continued and worsened, and the patient eventually filed a medical malpractice claim against the otolaryngologist, alleging failure to diagnose a severe inner ear infection.

The claim was ultimately dismissed when the plaintiffs lawyer could not locate an otolaryngological expert witness willing to testify the otolaryngologist committed medical negligence, and I therefore asked the plaintiffs lawyer why the patient filed a claim when it seemed clear the otolaryngologist did not commit medical negligence. The patient, who truly suffered the symptoms and complaints, was apparently so angry with the otolaryngologist for the manner in which he treated her—in the patient's words, "rudely and brusquely, walking into the examining room with his head buried in a file, not saying hello, roughly pushing my head from side to side instead of asking me to move it or gently tilting it himself, standing in the doorway with his head down writing something and then snapping at me not to interrupt him when I just asked him what he thought the problem was, snapping at me when I politely asked him to repeat what he said because I couldn't hear it due to the ringing in my ears"—that she insisted pursuing the claim even though no expert witness within the same specialty could be located. Despite the fact the claim was eventually dismissed, for nearly a year the otolaryngologist had to endure the stress of a pending medical malpractice claim, and had to deal with plaintiffs lawyers, defense attorneys, expert witnesses and a judge, simply because he exuded such a negative and offensive manner.

Every time I conduct the deposition of a plaintiff, I ask her why she is suing the health care provider I represent. In cases where that health care provider—my client—is not the main target of the lawsuit and may have been only peripherally involved in the plaintiff's care, the plaintiff's response oftentimes is that my client acted in a rude, offensive, disrespectful or arrogant manner. Whether physician or nurse, radiologic technician or orderly, medical student or laboratory assistant, health care providers are constantly named as defendants in medical malpractice claims based on how a patient feels they treated her. Even if you are ultimately dismissed from the lawsuit, don't increase the chances of having a claim filed against you because of your negative professional manner or poor patient interaction.

Obviously, the most important aspect of your care and treatment of a patient is the actual quality of care that patient receives from you and the rest of the medical professionals treating her. Presumably you will always strive to deliver the highest standard of care you can to every patient you treat (unless you subscribe to the theory of practicing *defensive medicine* in an effort never to get sued—defensive medicine is discussed in Chapter 2); however, it's the manner in which you deliver that care and treatment that may very well determine whether a medical malpractice claim is ever filed against you. No matter how pressed for time you may be or whatever other factors may exist, your most important patient is the one you're with at that very moment, and you must do all you can to ensure that patient feels as such.

| **Real World Example:** | *Subsequent to prescription of medication for high blood* |

pressure and medication for increased cholesterol that— according to the Physician's Desk Reference—*were contraindicated due to their adverse interaction, the prescribing physician telephoned me regarding his fear the patient would file a medical malpractice claim against him. The patient had suffered renal failure—just as the* PDR *warned—and nearly died while traveling abroad. The physician admitted he did not verify the potential contraindication before prescribing the two medications. As the physician was uninsured and thus personally responsible for any judgment rendered against him, he was understandably concerned. However, the patient simply told the physician she knew he was just trying his best and had always treated her with "polite respect" and therefore she saw no reason to "make a fuss," despite permanent, severe renal problems directly attributable to the physician's negligence. The patient never filed a medical malpractice claim, and she continued to treat with the physician.*

Unfortunately, there are no statistics regarding how many potential medical malpractice claims are avoided due to patients' respect and/or friendly affection for their health care providers, but based on personal experience and anecdotal evidence from both health care providers and legal colleagues, I have no doubt such is the leading preventative tool in precluding the filing of medical malpractice claims. The Harvard study noted in Chapter B—which found that less than three percent of patient injuries/deaths caused by negligent or substandard medical care resulted in medical malpractice claims ever being filed—may very well substantiate such an assertion.

From the patient's standpoint, the most awkward and potentially embarrassing aspect of receiving medical care oftentimes is the physical examination. A patient's sense of dignity and self-control may be compromised by disrobing in front of strangers, contorting her body into unseemly or even painful positions, being touched in personal, private areas. Patients require an adequate level of privacy in which to endure this most invasive of personal exposures, and whatever you can do to protect a patient's dignity and privacy can be invaluable in creating a positive, or at least neutral, experience for the patient. You, of course, must conduct a thorough physical examination (with an attendant present for genital exams and P/Es where the patient disrobes) and document such, but remember how the patient most likely perceives the experience, and the potential for humiliation, resentment or anger, possibly directed at you. In general, a patient is far more likely to consider filing a claim if she recalls the physical examination experience as intensely negative, degrading, disrespectful or unjustifiably painful. Even something as simple as knocking on the examination room door and then pausing a few seconds before entering displays the respect and courtesy patients crave, and may be the difference between a positive and negative patient impression.

Real World Fact: *Research indicates that whether medical malpractice cases are tried by juries or by the presiding judges ("bench trials") dollar damages awards are similar, but judges actually rule against defendant health care providers more frequently than juries do.*

Despite your best efforts to provide the highest quality care you possibly can—in a polite, professional manner—your patient may never understand or comprehend those efforts. Considering a patient's lack of knowledge regarding the practice of medicine, and the effects of the patient's condition and/or medications, it is remarkable a patient ever truly recognizes and appreciates the care and treatment she receives. Communication experts agree that approximately 55% of face-to-face communication comes from visual body language and 38% from voice, but a mere 7% of face-to-face communication derives from actual words. You may be using the right words with a patient, but what you're *communicating* to that patient and what she understands may be entirely contrary to what you intend.

Listen to your patient—the average physician interrupts a patient merely 17 seconds into the patient's description of the complaint—and then summarize or paraphrase what she told you; this not only communicates that you listened to her but also that your goal is to obtain a correct history so as to provide the best possible treatment course. Communicate openly, honestly and politely throughout the patient encounter, in both providing and receiving information. Finish the patient encounter strongly, leaving a positive final impression by reviewing the treatment plan, assuring the patient understands and agrees with that plan, and then asking the patient if there is anything else you can do for her. Close the visit with a genuine request the patient contact you with any questions or concerns and then, if appropriate, offer a friendly handshake or touch on the shoulder.

The essential element for the patient in the doctor-patient relationship is that the patient actually feels the doctor's concern and believes the doctor wants to help her. Not only does the patient need to receive appropriate medical care, she needs to *feel* she is receiving appropriate medical care. Your patient most likely does not understand all the tests and procedures she's enduring, why all the blood needs to be drawn, the urine samples repeatedly handed over, the unfamiliar faces of a new shift of doctors and nurses scanning her medical chart and asking her strange yet redundant questions. But she does understand her doctor appearing to listen to her, her doctor's reassurance and encouragement, her doctor's pleasant yet professional demeanor. Even if your personality is more stoic than engaging, more aloof than friendly, more professional than conversational, you can still practice positive patient communication by your manner, your body language and the tone of your voice.

Communication experts have found that, when two people meet for the first time, each typically judges the other within 10 seconds, usually based predominantly on non-verbal communication. In other words, when you walk into an examination room with your head down reading the intake sheet, by the time you look up your patient has already made an evaluation of you that will most likely continue throughout the course of the doctor-patient relationship. You cannot allow such a seemingly insignificant detail as negative body language or a bad first impression to be the impetus, the push that gets the patient over the hump, transforming her into a plaintiff and you into a medical malpractice defendant.

Real World Suggestions:

• *if at all possible, review the chart before entering the patient's room, not as you enter or in the hallway where the patient can watch you merely glance at it (your patient wants to feel valued, not as if you spent only a few seconds hurriedly skimming what, to her, is the most important information you will read that day)*

• *smile and make eye contact; if you feel comfortable doing so, shake the patient's hand (some health care providers even hug or embrace their long-time patients)*

• *if there is something personal you know about the patient or can discern from her appearance, briefly comment on or ask about it, and note it in the patient's chart so you can mention it again in the future; this will help put the patient at ease, establish rapport, and will better assist you with open communication*

• *inquire about the problem that necessitated the visit, not a generic "How are you feeling?"; this conveys to the patient that you have read her information or, even better from the patient's perspective, spoken to another health care provider about her*

• *some patients are talkers, while others will only respond with a "yes" or "no;" quickly determine your type of patient and communicate in a manner calculated to garner the most accurate and complete information (thousands of medical malpractice lawsuits have been filed based on a patient's assertion that the health care provider did not specifically ask about each and every symptom and/or complaint; see* Real World Example, *page 70)*

• *in general, don't write in the chart or dictate your notes until after you leave the examining room (a patient will often react negatively to a few terse, dictated phrases about herself when, to the patient, her condition is much more important or severe); if you have to write in the chart in front of a patient or type your notes into a laptop/computer, a simple "excuse me" is both polite and shows you want to concentrate on her when she is speaking, which goes a long way toward making a patient feel valued;*

to reinforce patient communication that occurred during the visit, some physicians dictate their notes—or verbally summarize while they're writing/typing their notes—in front of the patient and then ask if the patient understood what was dictated (such a technique can be a useful time-saving device if you adequately explain it and the patient clearly comprehends both the technique and the medical communication)

• conduct a thorough physical examination while providing the patient as much privacy, dignity and individual control as possible; attempt to have an attendant present; fully and completely document all aspects and findings of the physical examination in the patient's medical records (plaintiffs lawyers typically review the P/E records very carefully, hoping the physician failed to check all systems, did not adequately document all findings or simply missed something)

• a patient in the pre-op area awaiting the administration of anesthesia feels at her most vulnerable and frightened; reassure her that the procedure you planned and discussed with her in your office is about to occur and that everything is going according to plan; your confidence and reassurance will be directly felt by the patient

• even if you are a health care provider with little patient contact (i.e., pathologist, radiologist, anesthesiologist, laboratory technician, etc.), you must do what you can in your few patient encounters— whether in person, via telephone or in writing—to convey a professional yet open, caring demeanor; the fewer patient/family encounters you have, the more important they are [If you have questions about your particular medical practice or specialty, Appendix B lists resources for supplemental materials regarding specific practice areas and medical specialties.]

When communicating with a patient, speak clearly, simply and slowly, utilizing language and terminology the patient can understand. A 2006 report by the National Center for Educational Statistics found that less than one in six American adults could be classified as "proficient" regarding health/medical literacy (e.g., thousands of patients have mistakenly believed they had cancer because a physician told them their biopsy results were "negative" or the patient didn't understand the term "benign"). In law school, future attorneys learn that the average American juror has a ninth-grade education, and trial lawyers are taught to communicate at that level when in front of a jury. Err on the side of over-simplification in your patient communications; remember that your patient is not a professional colleague, that she may be scared or disoriented, but that she has an intense desire and vested personal interest in understanding what you're saying. Never condescend, but until you know that patient well enough to be absolutely certain how to speak to her, assume she has at best a ninth-grade education and communicate with her accordingly.

If, as some studies indicate, as few as 17 percent of all medical malpractice claims involve injuries actually caused by medical negligence or substandard care, then approximately 83 percent of medical malpractice lawsuits may involve care and treatment that was not substandard or negligent. As detailed in Chapter B, something other than medical negligence induced those patients to file a medical malpractice claim. You absolutely cannot allow your personality, your body language, the manner in which you communicate with patients, to be a predominant, or even minor, factor in a patient's decision whether to file a medical malpractice claim, especially in the 83 percent of occasions no medical negligence occurred.

Considering that factors most often cited as reasons patients initiate medical malpractice claims focus on a lack of honest, effective communication between patient and health care provider, the natural reaction of a health care provider to the prospect of being sued is the exact opposite behavior that should be exercised. When anyone faces the possibility of being sued, typically the first instinct is to clam up—to be silent and simply walk away in an attempt to distance oneself from the situation; but, considering the predominant reasons claims are filed in the first place, this natural reaction of silence and distance may be the most detrimental approach to an adverse medical incident. Numerous studies have shown that active disclosure and open lines of communication subsequent to adverse medical incidents actually decrease the likelihood a patient will initiate a medical malpractice claim. In fact, one study revealed that after a hospital instituted a policy of open, active patient disclosure subsequent to adverse medical incidents, the rate of medical malpractice claims declined. Forthright communication with patients may reduce medical malpractice claims by decreasing patients' feelings of helplessness, confusion and resentment, reducing the chances they will ever contact a plaintiffs lawyer to explore filing a claim.

The University of Michigan Health System began a program in 2002 aimed at reducing medical malpractice claims through effective physician-patient communication. The program sought to identify cases in which a patient suffered injury due to a confirmed medical error and compensate those patients quickly and fairly. By 2005 the number of medical malpractice claims dropped by more than half, and the health system was actually able to increase the number of physicians and faculty members in neurosurgery, obstetrics/gynecology and other high-risk fields. Other major hospitals (e.g., Johns Hopkins, Dana Farber Cancer Institute, Children's Hospital and Clinics Minneapolis-St. Paul, the Veterans Administration of Lexington, Kentucky) have also initiated similar policies of "extreme honesty."

If you're employed by a hospital, medical facility, health care system or medical office, prior to discussing an adverse medical incident with your patient or her family, verify with a risk manager, supervisor, administrator or your malpractice insurer the procedure for patient communication when you believe such an incident has occurred. Although medical malpractice laws and the legal consequences of a physician's statements differ vastly from state to state, remember that open, honest discussions most likely will prevent more medical malpractice claims than such communication will engender. Chapter 6 elucidates on what to say, and what not to say, when discussing an adverse medical incident.

2

A Chart, A Chart, My Kingdom for a Chart
Medical Records

A doctor who cannot take a good history and a patient who cannot give one are in danger of giving and receiving bad treatment.
—Anonymous

The medical chart, as every physician and health care provider knows, is the single most important component in providing continuity of care. Without it, doctors and nurses, technicians and therapists, assistants and orderlies have no idea what course of treatment, medications, tests, procedures or surgeries are to be performed, have actually been performed, or what progress or lack thereof has been made. The chart is the lifeblood of a patient's care; without it, the medical team treating her is lost.

But the chart is also the lifeblood of another professional team—the medical malpractice plaintiffs lawyer's firm. The single most important piece of evidence to any plaintiffs lawyer suing you will be the chart—your patient's chart, his client's chart. To you, the chart means one thing; to the plaintiffs lawyer, it means something entirely different. This is not to suggest what you write in the chart should be anything other than exactly what you were taught in medical school, anything other than what prudent medical care dictates. However, you absolutely must know that in a medical malpractice lawsuit, the chart comprises nearly all the documentary evidence a plaintiffs lawyer utilizes when attempting to prove medical negligence in the care and treatment of his client, your former patient.

Real World Fact: *Every state allows a patient some form of access to her own medical records; there is no legal way to prevent a patient such access. If a facility or health care provider does attempt to prevent a patient from accessing her own medical records, it/he may be charged with a crime and/or sued by the patient for failure to provide access to medical records, depending on the state in which the violation occurs.*

After a patient contacts a medical malpractice plaintiffs lawyer and they meet to discuss a potential claim, the first thing a plaintiffs lawyer will do if he is considering taking the case is request a copy of the medical chart. No other profession provides a chronological blow-by-blow history that allows expert witnesses, judges and jurors in a subsequent lawsuit to determine exactly what happened, if someone in fact did commit medical negligence and what damages were sustained due to that medical negligence. To prevent a medical malpractice claim from ever being filed, you want to ensure there is nothing in those medical records to whet a plaintiffs lawyer's appetite; you want him to listen to your former patient, read through the medical records himself, and then politely say she has no case. Understanding the medical chart from this differing perspective will allow you to place as much emphasis and importance on the chart as judges and jurors do, and as you should.

Real World Example: In a medical malpractice case involving the death of a patient during a post-op hospital stay subsequent to routine abdominal surgery, the defendants—the attending physician, the surgeon, the nurses and the hospital—were all forced to settle the case prior to trial based simply on the medical records. Instead of improving post-surgery, the patient slowly deteriorated over the course of six days until she expired (from sepsis, according to the pathology report), despite the fact no complications were noted in the surgical record and no cause of deterioration was noted in the chart. The patient was seen every day post-op by the surgeon and the attending physician, as well as receiving constant nursing care. Several times the attending physician and surgeon noted in the chart that there was no known cause for the patient's deteriorating condition. The nurses continually charted the patient's vital signs and data, including detailed records of fluid intake and output ("I & O").

After a medical malpractice claim was filed for the wrongful death of the patient, the expert witness retained by the plaintiffs lawyer to review the medical records immediately issued a report stating the death could have been prevented if only the health care providers had actually read the medical chart. Clear from any subsequent reading of the chart was that the patient was "free spacing" (taking in and retaining far more liquid than excreting); therefore, a perforation must have occurred in the stomach wall and the patient leaked stomach fluid through the perforation into the abdominal cavity, resulting in the patient's infection. The nurses' detailed records of "I & O" showed that for six days the patient's fluid intake was far greater than output. The only evidence the malpractice plaintiffs lawyer needed to prove his case was that nurses' record of fluid intake and output. Had either the attending physician or surgeon simply read and comprehended what was occurring, or if a nurse had just pointed it out to the physicians, the patient most likely would not have died. In this case, the chart proved the medical negligence so clearly that no trial was necessary in order for the family of the deceased patient to recover.

ه above case exemplifies the need for physicians
th care providers to review, at least periodically, the
medical chart. If five years after the fact, a juror with no
medical training can easily glean from the chart that which
should have been patently obvious to the health care
providers actually treating the patient if the health care
providers simply read the chart, that juror will want not
only to render a verdict in favor of the plaintiff, he most
likely will also want to punish the health care provider who
rendered the negligent medical care. Cases such as these
typically result in high dollar jury awards.

Jurors don't want to hear about the time demands
placed on health care providers, about the voluminous
medical records that would take hours to sift through,
about doctors not routinely reading nursing notes or
detailed patient histories; every single person sitting on that
jury will be a past or future patient—not a doctor, or nurse
or health care provider. And what may be a legitimate
explanation why the physician did not read the medical
chart (e.g., "I rely on my nurses to read the records and
communicate verbally any pertinent information to me")
simply will not fly with a jury. If a patient has a problem
you don't understand, one of the many tasks you must
perform is to review the medical chart—or risk sitting in
front of a jury in a medical malpractice trial explaining why
you didn't.

Real World Numbers: *The average verdict
rendered by a jury in a medical malpractice trial is
$4,700,000. The average pre-trial settlement in a medical
malpractice lawsuit is $1,000,000.*

Nearly every physician, nurse, dentist, chiropractor,
podiatrist, physician assistant, nurse anesthetist, lab
technician, phlebotomist, therapist and every other type of
health care practitioner knows the phrase by heart: *if you
didn't write it down, you didn't do it.* Nowhere is that
maxim more accurate than in the world of medical
malpractice claims. No matter how true his words, when a
doctor sits on the witness stand and tells a jury he really

did speak with a specialist regarding the patient's condition despite the fact there is no notation in the medical chart of such consult, the jury most likely will not believe him, especially when that same doctor just testified that it is both hospital policy and proper medical procedure to notate any such consults in the medical records. Plaintiffs lawyers—and jurors—usually believe that what is written in the medical records represents exactly what happened in the course of a patient's treatment, and that if something is not written down in the chart as actually occurring then it simply did not happen, no matter how much verbal testimony that it did.

When that patient does contact a medical malpractice plaintiffs lawyer and the two of them are sitting in the lawyer's office, as his legal assistant—who may be a former nurse or physician assistant—pores over a copy of the medical records, what that plaintiffs lawyer wants to find in the chart is some glaring piece of evidence, a "smoking gun" that shouts out: no result for a test that was ordered can be found in the chart; a lab value was noted outside the normal range without an explanation; a medication prescribed by the physician was never written off by a nurse. These are the kind of "charting" mistakes that can lead to a medical malpractice claim being filed against you, despite the fact you know in your heart and have a clear recollection that someone told you the results of that test, that there is a logical explanation why the lab value fell outside the normal range, that you actually watched the nurse administer the medication you ordered. Don't find yourself a defendant in a medical malpractice lawsuit, even though you rendered perfectly appropriate care, simply because the chart does not reflect that you in fact provided appropriate care.

Real World Example: | *A pediatrician—who was extremely dedicated and thorough, was highly regarded by both the community and his peers, and had never had any type of claim or lawsuit filed against him in all his years of practice—began treating a patient when she was 15 months old, seeing her at least once a year for the next four years. On each visit the* *pediatrician examined the patient, ordered all appropriate tests and documented his findings in the medical records. The patient did not suffer any symptoms or complaints other than those typically experienced during childhood, but during each visit the patient's mother noted that the patient's limbs appeared to be growing at a non-uniform rate. After measuring the child's limbs himself and determining a bilateral difference in limb size, the pediatrician made a note of such in the chart, and again did so when the mother mentioned that fact on three subsequent visits. Finally, when the patient was five and a half years old, the pediatrician decided to request an orthopedic consult to assist in determining why the patient's limbs were not growing uniformly. The orthopedist immediately identified the patient's condition as hemihypertrophy.*

When the patient was subsequently diagnosed with Wilm's Tumor, the patient's mother filed a medical malpractice claim against the pediatrician, alleging failure to timely diagnose the hemihypertrophy. The case had to be settled, as the pediatrician's own office chart clearly showed that on each visit the patient's limbs were not growing at a uniform rate, yet the pediatrician did nothing. His only explanation for failing to act was that he was too busy to read over the patient's chart prior to each visit and therefore did not know the patient's limbs were not growing uniformly. Initially, the pediatrician blamed managed care for placing him in the position of not having ample time to review the chart prior to examining the patient; however, he now reports that he reads over the entire office chart before seeing each and every patient and has not had any other malpractice claims filed against him. His office practice has not suffered financially due to his added diligence, and in fact he reports it operates more smoothly and efficiently.

Proper documentation not only results in decreasing the chances you will be sued for medical malpractice, it improves patient care. As you well know, in most hospital settings the chart is the primary—or in many cases the only—manner in which health care providers communicate with each other. Only in the most unique of cases do the nursing staff, attending physician, radiologist, surgeon and/or other specialists actually discuss a patient together. What is written in the chart subsists as the conversation, consult and entire context of communication and decision of the medical team caring for that patient, as far as a plaintiffs lawyer or malpractice jury is concerned. Other health care providers—and defense attorneys—may well know such is not the case, but defense attorneys are not the ones who decide whether you are sued for medical malpractice.

      With all this being said, there is an inapposite maxim, the other side of the coin that is essential to providing proper patient care: *don't treat the chart, treat the patient.* The last thing a defense attorney, or a patient, or your own sense of medical responsibility and ethics wants is for you to be so concerned about proper charting that you neglect treating the patient, that you in fact render substandard or negligent medical care simply so that you can chart properly. I have won enough cases where the health care provider rendered perfectly appropriate care despite the fact the chart did not reflect appropriate care to know that jurors can indeed understand when a doctor does everything he can but it simply isn't enough. But a defense attorney can't do a whole lot to help you when you render obviously negligent medical care resulting in an injured patient, despite the fact your charting is immaculate. Always treat the patient; just do your best to have the chart reflect that.

Defensive Medicine:

Some health care providers have begun to practice "defensive medicine" in the face of increased malpractice insurance premiums and fear of being sued. They order every test imaginable—even if the test could negatively impact the patient—simply so they can defend their care as thorough and appropriate in any subsequent litigation. These health care providers chart impeccably, appearing to the uninitiated as thoroughly competent practitioners. One study found that as many as 55% of physicians reported their medical decisions were "extremely" or "very" influenced by their desire to reduce the chances of being sued for malpractice.   A detailed survey of "high-risk" Pennsylvania physicians published in the Journal of the American Medical Association *found that 93% reported practicing some form of defensive medicine: 59% reported often ordering more diagnostic tests than were medically indicated; 52% reported often referring patients to other specialists in unnecessary circumstances; 43% reported using imaging technology in clinically unnecessary circumstances; 42% reported taking steps to restrict their practice, such as avoiding patients with complex medical problems or eliminating certain procedures such as trauma surgery; 33% reported often prescribing more medications than medically were indicated; 33% reported recommending invasive procedures that were medically unnecessary.*

Providing appropriate patient care is the best way to minimize the possibility of being sued, not ordering every test under the sun or sloughing your patient off onto another physician.   Following your medical education, training, experience, instincts and the suggestions in this book are the ways to preclude a medical malpractice claim, not ordering unnecessary diagnostic procedures or canceling risky but necessary surgeries.   Health care providers typically choose their profession for the most traditional and personal of reasons: "Wherever the art of medicine is loved, there also is love of humanity." (Hippocrates).   No book has to tell you the primary and most important focus of your medical practice is your patient, not practicing defensive medicine in an attempt to avoid being sued.   A physician who practices defensive medicine may one day be forced either to lie under oath, or respond in front of a jury that the reason he ordered a particular test or prescribed a specific course of treatment was simply so he would not be sued.   If such testimony does not cause a medical malpractice jury to render a massive award against a physician, nothing will.

When utilizing medical abbreviations, ensure all health care providers know exactly what the abbreviations mean.   Every physician, resident, nurse and medical student may well know that "HEENT" stands for "Head, Eyes, Ears, Nose, Throat" and "SOAP" stands for "Subjective, Objective, Assessment, Plan," but there are potentially hundreds of abbreviations that are particular to a specific practice, specialty, discipline or geographic area; even within a specialty there may be conflicting abbreviations. Don't get caught in a situation where you intend one thing by utilizing a particular abbreviation but the health care provider reading your abbreviation interprets something entirely different.

I once conducted a seminar for physicians and nurses from different parts of the country wherein I wrote various medical abbreviations on a blackboard and asked the physicians and nurses to identify what the abbreviations meant. For every single abbreviation in my makeshift example, the health care providers at the seminar offered at least three different opinions as to what the abbreviation meant, on some occasions offering up to six different opinions what the abbreviation meant. Simply put, you cannot assume you understand another health care provider's abbreviation, nor can you assume another health care provider understands yours. Even if you practice in the same setting every day alongside the same health care providers who utilize the exact same abbreviations, be aware that a patient's medical records may end up with a consultant, specialist or subsequent health care provider who has no idea what you really mean by a particular abbreviation. If you have any doubts whatsoever about a medical abbreviation, pick up the phone and call that health care provider, or write a letter or e-mail; document such communication in the chart. The practice of medicine may necessitate the use of abbreviations, but you must be certain everyone knows what those abbreviations mean.

Real World Example: *Upon the advice of their attending obstetrician, an expectant couple sought consultation at a genetics center due to the fact they were blood-related first cousins. The geneticist subsequently recommended an alpha fetal protein "triple screen" to test for possible genetic abnormalities, specifically Down's Syndrome; the geneticist made the recommendation by noting "Recommend AFP[3]" on the genetics center consult form. The couple took the consult* *form back to their obstetrician, who worked at the free clinic where the couple received prenatal care. The obstetrician had never previously seen the abbreviation "AFP³" and therefore performed only an alpha fetal protein test (a "single screen"). The single screen was interpreted as negative for any abnormalities and the couple proceeded with the pregnancy, subsequently giving birth to a daughter with Down's Syndrome.*

The couple sued both the obstetrician and the free clinic, and ultimately the genetics center and the geneticist, for medical malpractice, alleging negligent failure to diagnose Down's Syndrome; at the time of the incident, a triple screen was considered approximately 80%-90% accurate in predicting Down's Syndrome, a single screen only 45%-60% accurate. As the obstetrician admitted he did not know what "AFP³" meant other than opining that it could have meant to perform a single screen three times, the free clinic and obstetrician were forced to settle their portion of the lawsuit. Despite the fact the genetics center had been utilizing the abbreviation "AFP³" to signify a triple screen for over a year, the genetics center and geneticist were similarly forced to settle their portion of the lawsuit when the plaintiffs lawyer located a geneticist from another state who testified "AFP³" was not a generally accepted abbreviation for a triple screen such that a free clinic should know what it meant. If the geneticist had simply written "triple screen" or the obstetrician had telephoned, written or e-mailed the genetics center for an explanation, the entire case may have been avoided, as opposed to settling on the eve of trial.

The above case may appear extreme, but consider it from the standpoint of a plaintiffs lawyer, the one who is deciding whether to take the case. Had the geneticist simply written "triple screen" as opposed to "AFP³," he and the genetics center would never have been sued, as the sole allegation of negligence against them was inaccurate communication of the recommendation. In fact, the geneticist and genetics center were only added to the lawsuit subsequent to the obstetrician testifying at his deposition that he did not know what "AFP³" meant. When the plaintiffs lawyer heard that testimony, his first thought certainly must have been how to bring the genetics center and geneticist into the lawsuit, increasing the number of "pockets" from which he could seek damages. The geneticist knew the patient was going to take the consult form from the genetics center to a free clinic, and should have known there was at least a possibility a physician not practicing within a genetics center would be unaware what the abbreviation meant. Had the geneticist written "triple screen" instead of "AFP³," not only would a lawsuit have been avoided, a triple screen may have in fact been performed and read as positive for Down's Syndrome, providing the expectant couple the opportunity to decide whether to proceed with the pregnancy. Reducing the possibility of having a medical malpractice claim filed against you oftentimes also results in improved medical care.

Real World Suggestions:

• *document your preliminary and differential diagnosis—including your medical reasoning— ensuring you note your clinical judgment in the chart (this not only provides an explanation in the records why treatment proceeded in a particular manner, but it will also serve to remind you years later why you made such a decision and may, from a simple review of the chart, convince a plaintiffs lawyer's expert witness that your clinical reasoning/medical judgment was sound and therefore no grounds exist to file a malpractice claim); the chart should reflect both what you did and why you did it, why you chose one treatment modality over another; ensure any operative or surgical notes adequately explain your intra-operative findings and why you undertook the specific actions or inactions intra-operatively*

• *document all discussions with colleagues, specialists, consultants, attendings, etc., even if they do not occur in a setting where the chart is readily available; this will not only help prevent medical malpractice claims, it will refresh your recollection why you chose a particular differential diagnosis or course of treatment (if you* are a resident, documenting your discussions with attendings and supervising residents will verify you appropriately discussed the case with superiors)

• document all discussions with patients, especially those where you discuss potential risks and complications and where you explain patient responsibilities; note who else is present for these discussions (e.g., family members, other health care providers, etc.), which may bolster your defense if you are sued—the patient will have difficulty asserting you never told her something when it is documented in the chart that you not only told the patient but her family as well; and, another health care provider may more readily recall the conversation when he reads in the chart he was present

• document telephone conversations, and consider creating a routine record of all calls via a pre-printed form you keep next to every telephone in your office/facility (and your home, car, etc.)

• document patients' cancellations of appointments, testing, procedures and all occasions the patient does something to jeopardize the treatment course or result (this shows if care/treatment did not occur it was at the patient's behest and not yours, and may even show the patient as being non-compliant and failing to follow a recommended treatment course or ignoring medical advice)

• make chart entries in a timely manner (don't wait until the end of your shift), ensure you not only date your notes but time them as well, and make chart entries in chronological order; do not leave empty space between notes such that someone could mistakenly chart information out of chronological order

• dictate discharge summaries on the day of discharge to ensure events are most clearly recollected and information fresh/current

• document only factual information, but if you need to include information garnered from another source ensure you cite that source (e.g., "Patient's spouse bedside, reports 'severe coughing and convulsions at 8:00 pm,' but not observed by medical personnel")

- *chart objectively, not subjectively* (e.g., "Patient states 'I fell on my way to the bathroom'" not "Patient fell on way to bathroom"; "surgical site healing, no signs of infection" not "wound O.K.")

- *do not make personal or derogatory comments in the chart, other than to record personally observed occurrences/incidents (e.g., "Patient's spouse stated to me in loud voice, 'You are incompetent'" not "wife nasty and shouting")*

- *print out any e-mails or letters you write or receive regarding a patient and place them in the chart; not only does this provide evidence of the communication, it will assist you in recalling the course and scope of care and treatment and why you chose one over another*

- *ensure copies of any external records or documents (e.g., letters, other health care providers' records, hospital paperwork, laboratory results, radiologic reports, consults, etc.) are placed in the chart, and consider stamping or initialing them as received, along with the date*

- *ensure all written records have a back-up copy, and all electronic records have a hard copy back-up*

- *never, ever alter a medical record; if you make a mistake,· simply draw one line through the previous entry and make a corrected entry above, below or after it, ensuring you date the correction, and/or follow the procedures and guidelines established at the facilities where you practice [In rare instances, defendant health care providers are accused of altering medical records by writing additional or substitute notes in the chart after the fact; plaintiffs lawyers use every means available, including the latest technology and ink testing/dating, to determine if records have been altered or added to and when: even if well-intended, do not alter medical records—only correct mistakes via proper procedure.]*

- *ensure you have not only performed but thoroughly documented a complete physical examination where appropriate; the notes of your P/E should portray you as professional, conscientious and detailed (thorough, detailed notes of the initial patient encounter can immediately convince a plaintiffs lawyer you are both professional and proficient and therefore unlikely to have committed a medical error—plaintiffs lawyers are human, too, and oftentimes go by their first impressions)*

- *document as much objective information as possible regarding your patient and patient's history, which not only serves to provide detailed information potentially useful in your diagnosis and treatment but also may assist in preventing a malpractice claim: plaintiffs lawyers often refuse potential malpractice cases based on negative information generated by the plaintiff within the medical records, so consider creating a comprehensive patient questionnaire/self-assessment form that not only provides you and other health care providers historical information but also allows the patient—if she possesses negative personality traits or is prone to exaggeration—to self-document potentially damaging information in the medical records (e.g., a patient who completes a self-assessment form noting "10" on a pain scale over an extended period of time will have difficulty convincing a jury the pain your alleged malpractice caused her is any worse than her previous pain; or, a patient who writes voluminous, non-sensical criticisms of previous health care providers may be viewed by jurors as having some type of persecution complex, or simply as an incessant complainer—plaintiffs lawyers realize this and are thus less likely to accept her case)*

- *never utilize the medical records as your personal "CYA"—to employ a common abbreviation—defense (e.g., avoid blaming phrases such as "neurosurgeon paged four times but never appeared for consult"; never use terms such as* stupid, incompetent, negligent, wrong, *etc.)*

- *ensure uniformity of abbreviations in your office and institutions; don't get caught in the trap of chart miscommunication simply because you utilize one abbreviation to represent something and the hospital utilizes a different abbreviation to represent the same thing*

- *instruct all new personnel in the use and meaning of abbreviations, and establish office or facility procedures whereby abbreviations coming from or going to outside facilities can be verified*

> • *if possible, produce and disseminate pamphlets or other documentation reflecting changes or updates to terms and abbreviations, as well as advances or updates for testing and procedures; distribute these materials throughout your geographic practice area*

> • *write as legibly as possible; jurors won't care that your nurse can read your handwriting, they want to be able to read it themselves; tens of thousands of medical malpractice claims result from poorly written or misunderstood prescriptions, orders, recommendations, etc. (e.g., "D/C" is intended as "Discharge" but mistaken as "Discontinue," and when followed by a list of medications they are mistakenly discontinued)*

> • *consider fully writing out commonly mistaken terms (e.g., "daily" rather than "Q.D.") and capitalizing portions of terms/medications that may be easily confused (e.g., "predNISONE" and "predNISOLONE," "clomiPHENE" and "clomiPRAMINE," "DOBUTamine" and "DOPamine," etc.), or, if you believe in the efficacy of such systems, suggest your facility consider using a Computer Physician Order Entry to help reduce medication errors that occur at the prescribing and/or order-filling stage by reducing confusion regarding the identification and use of prescriptions*

In medical malpractice lawsuits that proceed to trial, the most frequent injury claimed is death (23%), followed by brain damage (9%), genital injuries (7%) and leg injuries (5%). Spinal/nerve injuries, cancer, and eye injuries each comprise four percent, amputations, paralysis, intestinal tract injuries and foot injuries each three percent, and other injuries total three percent.

3

Talk, Talk, Talk, Talk—Please
Medical Communications

No doctor is better than three.
—German Proverb

Physicians and health care providers must effectively communicate with the other members of the medical team treating a patient—or risk providing substandard care while simultaneously increasing the possibility of being sued for medical malpractice. Attendings, surgeons, specialists, residents, nurses, technicians and therapists comprise the medical team, yet it is rare they all meet to discuss a patient's condition, treatment and progress. Lack of communication with the other health care providers treating a patient leads not only to potentially substandard care, but can be a relatively easy case for a medical malpractice plaintiffs lawyer to prosecute. Even if health care providers cannot meet in person to discuss a patient's care, they absolutely must exercise effective communication techniques to ensure appropriate care is rendered, and that such appropriate care is documented and can thus be defended in the event of an adverse medical incident.

A vast number of medical malpractice cases I defend center on health care providers simply not communicating important information to one another; an injury or fatality should not have occurred but did merely because, even though pertinent, vital information was available, it was not timely relayed to the appropriate health care provider. Invariably, the negligent health care provider seeks to blame managed care or the health care system, or a lack of proper communication procedure at the particular facility; these defenses accomplish nothing and instead tend to anger jurors. Patients—both those you treat and those who sit as jurors in medical malpractice trials—want to know that doctors and nurses talk to each other, tell each other what's occurring with a patient's care, discuss prognosis and treatment, and have the time and professional expertise to ensure that all relevant information regarding a patient is thoroughly communicated, not simply written in the chart without an appropriate verbal alert when necessary.

Real World Example: *A patient presented to a hospital on the day of her scheduled urologic procedure, wherein an intake nurse conducted a history and pre-surgical questionnaire. The patient informed the nurse she had ingested aspirin within the past twelve hours, which the nurse noted on the questionnaire. The nurse placed the history and questionnaire in the medical chart, which was immediately available to the urologic surgeon. The urologic surgeon talked with the patient prior to the administration of anesthesia but did not specifically question her regarding medications taken; he never read the intake history or pre-surgical questionnaire. The procedure was performed without any complications and was considered a success, but post-operatively the patient experienced excessive bleeding, which was attributed to the patient's blood's inability to properly coagulate due to her ingestion of aspirin. The surgeon blamed the nurse for not orally communicating to him information he deemed crucial, which would have forced him to postpone the procedure; the nurse and hospital blamed the* *surgeon for not reading the history/questionnaire or questioning the patient himself.*

In a strikingly similar case, a middle-aged woman presented to a hospital on the morning of her scheduled gastric bypass surgery. An intake nurse verbally questioned the patient, eliciting the information that, during sexual intercourse a month prior, the patient experienced a severe headache, lost consciousness and was rushed to the ER. The intake nurse reported the information by writing "H/A one mo. prior, 10 on pain scale." The patient then met with the anesthesiologist, who had access to the completed intake form but neither read it nor questioned the patient regarding headaches. The patient underwent the procedure but never regained consciousness, instead dying from a ruptured brain aneurysm one day post-op. Her family sued the anesthesiologist, intake nurse, hospital and surgeon, alleging anesthesia should never have been administered due to the recent history of severe headache that in all medical probability was a "pre-bleed" to the fatal ruptured aneurysm. Had the intake nurse more accurately recorded the patient's description of the headache and brought such to the attention of the anesthesiologist, or had the anesthesiologist read the intake form or questioned the patient himself, the procedure would have been cancelled; the surgeon actually read the intake form but merely assumed the anesthesiologist had followed up with the patient. Had either the nurse and anesthesiologist or anesthesiologist and surgeon simply talked to each other, the patient might still be alive and a multi-million dollar jury award not rendered.

As pressed for time as health care providers are these days, it may be impossible for all members of the medical team to meet and discuss a patient's care, but two physicians can telephone each other, a doctor can talk directly to a nurse, a resident can page or e-mail his supervising resident/attending, an internist can grab a neurosurgeon in the hallway. To a medical malpractice jury, health care providers actually discussing a patient's care—as opposed to merely communicating via written words in the chart—goes a long way toward displaying a genuine degree of care, concern and professional expertise, and to providing appropriate care that jurors feel comfortable adjudging as within the standard of care. And any such discussions must absolutely be noted in the chart, not only for the reasons previously discussed in Chapter 2, but to provide continuity of care and a documented explanation why a specific treatment course was pursued.

> **Real World Numbers:** *Research regarding jury verdicts in medical malpractice lawsuits that progress to trial reveals that a plaintiff prevails against an individual physician defendant 30% of the time. When both an individual physician and a hospital/medical facility are defendants in a lawsuit, plaintiffs prevail at trial 35% of the time. Plaintiffs prevail at 50% of trials against hospitals, medical facilities or institutions.*

Physicians and other health care providers should not hesitate to consult medical personnel in other practice areas and disciplines—and even other health care providers within the same practice area—in determining diagnosis, prognosis or treatment modality. As the patient always comes first, such liberal attempts to garner additional medical opinions simply make sound medical sense and typically result in better, more thorough care; and, from a legal standpoint, the benefits are enormous. Whether a plaintiffs lawyer is deciding to accept a potential medical malpractice case or a defense attorney is preparing a health care provider's trial defense, few things look better for the defendant health care provider than consults with other physicians documented in the medical records.

Plaintiffs lawyers love it when—in a complex or difficult case—a physician tries to fly solo, allowing that plaintiffs lawyer to paint the physician as an arrogant would-be hero who neither needs nor accepts any opinion other than his own (some physicians refuse to even consider a suggestion from a non-physician health care provider, despite the suggestion being appropriate). Defense attorneys cringe, realizing the entire defense rests on a medical opinion made by and acted upon by a single physician. Such claims/lawsuits certainly are winnable for the health care provider, but if there is any question as to diagnosis or treatment modality, the plaintiffs lawyer will exercise wide latitude in depicting the physician as having a God complex, as one who would never stoop to consider another physician's or health care provider's opinion.

| *Real World Example:* | *A mother presented her two year old at a hospital's* |

emergency room, complaining the child was fussy, cried continuously, had a fever and had been vomiting. The child had an extensive medical history with the pediatric service at the hospital, of which the mother informed the ER nurses. A pediatric resident examined the child in the emergency room, ordered abdominal films—which were read as negative by an attending radiologist—and then discharged the child subsequent to his finding that the child merely had a gaseous stomach. The resident never consulted an attending pediatrician and never reviewed the child's pediatric records, which were readily available via hospital computer. A few hours later the mother returned to the ER with the child, who was in acute distress. An attending pediatric surgeon was immediately summoned and made heroic attempts to save the child, who unfortunately expired due to an intra-abdominal infection.

The hospital, resident and attending pediatric surgeon were sued for the wrongful death of the child, and were forced to settle the case prior to trial. The plaintiffs lawyer alleged—and could have easily proven at trial—that the resident committed medical negligence by discharging the child before first contacting an attending physician to confirm the diagnosis, and by not either reviewing the previous pediatric records or verbally contacting a pediatrician familiar with the child's care. The hospital and attending physician were alleged to have supervised the resident in a negligent manner—also a violation of the standard of care—by not properly ensuring the resident communicated with other medical personnel. The plaintiffs' expert witness opined the child would not have died had the resident not discharged her; I could find no expert witness willing to testify the resident did not commit medical negligence in discharging the child, nor could I find an expert witness willing to testify that inappropriately discharging the child was not the cause of death. This case was therefore deemed indefensible.

Although no empirical statistics exist documenting the specific allegations of medical malpractice cases filed across the country, from my own and colleagues' experiences it is safe to approximate a large percentage involve ineffective communication among members of the medical team. Even when a medical malpractice claim is not premised strictly on inadequate or ineffective medical communication, typically there is some communication component involved in most claims. It is therefore imperative health care providers comprehend the magnitude of effective communication in relation to the possibility of a medical malpractice claim being filed; from your own medical training and experience you are already well aware of the implications and consequences of ineffective communication in relation to providing appropriate medical care.

Real World Suggestions:

• *if at all possible, verbally discuss important medical issues with other members of the team and then immediately document such discussions in the chart; if you possess important information, ensure you communicate it verbally to other members of the medical team (in the world of medical malpractice claims, if one health care provider possesses vital information, it is virtually impossible to defend a case where knowledge of that information by another health care provider would have necessitated or precluded a procedure, surgery or treatment modality)*

• *enact an office or facility procedure whereby vital medical history or information is timely communicated verbally to the appropriate health care provider in addition to being written in the chart; such policy should include a procedure whereby the verbal communication is documented as having occurred*

- *talk to other members of the medical team prior to any surgery/procedure, especially if for some reason you do not read the intake form/questionnaire; train intake personnel to ask probing questions that help discern if there is any reason the surgery/procedure should not occur (many facilities utilize new hires or trainees as intake personnel—consider rotating veteran medical personnel in a supervisory or oversight capacity to verify intake procedures and ensure appropriate care and follow through by intake personnel)*

- *be thorough in your questioning of patients, as oftentimes patients do not volunteer information because they do not view it as relevant even though it is in fact crucial; anesthesiologists should be especially vigilant in both their pre-anesthesia questioning of patients and in their review of any intake form or questionnaire, including discussing with intake personnel anything at all questionable*

- *consider implementing a policy whereby anesthesiologists and surgeons must sign off as having read any intake form/questionnaire*

- *consider implementing a policy whereby laboratory results and values outside normal ranges (or any relevant results/values) are timely communicated directly to the appropriate health care provider*

- *liberally seek out other health care providers and specialists with whom to consult, especially in difficult, challenging or complex cases; document any discussions/recommendations in the medical records*

- *if consulted on a patient, don't simply read those portions of the medical records you initially believe to be relevant to your component of care, attempt to read as much of the entire chart as possible; ask the attending physician and other members of the medical team if there is anything you should know that might affect your consult/recommendations; ask pertinent questions of the medical team; document all discussions and communications in the medical records*

• *the two* Real World Examples *on pages 70 and 71 mirror the fictional medical malpractice case in the motion picture* The Verdict, *starring Paul Newman, wherein neither the obstetrician nor the anesthesiologist read the nurse's intake history, which noted the patient had consumed food within an hour previous to the emergency C-section the obstetrician performed; the patient was administered anesthesia, vomited into the mask and subsequently suffered irreversible brain damage; many of the film's courtroom and trial preparation scenes provide a relatively accurate glimpse of the realities of a medical malpractice case (but the depiction of a downtrodden plaintiffs lawyer with precious few resources battling the invincible defense law firm rings patently false; plaintiffs lawyers have nearly inexhaustible financial, personnel and professional resources and are formidable legal opponents— never underestimate them)*

4

In Golf, in Medicine, in Life— It's All About the Follow Through
Verifying It Gets Done

The physician should look upon the patient as a besieged city and try to rescue him with every means that art and science place at his command.
—Alexander of Tralles

How many times in your practice have you encountered a procedure that was ordered but never actually performed, a prescribed medication that was never given, a lab test requested but never completed? Whether you are the physician ordering a task be accomplished or the health care provider responsible for completing that task, you know full well that sometimes things simply don't get done. If ever there is a situation where plaintiffs lawyers are waiting, circling, panting, now you know what it is.

Unfortunately, in my practice I have seen literally hundreds of instances where a medication was never written off, no lab values in the chart for tests that were ordered, no results of a diagnostic procedure in the medical records despite a physician's order that one be performed. And regardless if the task was in truth performed, to the plaintiffs lawyer—and to most medical malpractice jurors—it simply never happened.

| **Real World Example:** | A *patient presented to an* |

oncologist after her primary care physician recommended a consult subsequent to discovering a mass in the patient's breast. The oncologist examined the patient and ordered an ultrasound, the results of which—interpreted by the radiologist as having malignant characteristics and therefore recommendation for biopsy—were forwarded to the oncologist. The oncologist sent to the patient, at the home address listed by the patient on her intake form, a letter requesting she contact the oncologist for the results. When the patient did not respond to the letter, the oncologist telephoned the home number listed by the patient on her intake form and spoke to the person who answered the phone, informing that person the patient should contact the oncologist immediately; the patient never contacted the oncologist, and the oncologist never attempted any further follow-up. The mass continued to grow until the patient eventually had it biopsied, the results of which revealed a malignancy.

The patient sued the oncologist, alleging failure to diagnose/delay in diagnosis. The case proceeded to trial, at which the jury rendered a massive award; the patient died less than a month after trial. The plaintiff's expert witnesses testified, and the jury apparently believed, that the oncologist committed medical negligence by not having a follow-up procedure in place that would increase effective communication between oncologist and patient regarding vital medical information. Although I still believe the jury was swayed by its sympathy for the dying plaintiff and that the oncologist did not in fact provide negligent medical care, subsequent to the verdict the oncologist enacted office procedures whereby a more thorough follow-up would be accomplished between himself and his patients. Since that time the oncologist has not been subjected to any medical malpractice claims and believes he now provides better patient care via improved doctor-patient communication procedures.

Real World Fact: *Whether a medical malpractice lawsuit proceeds to trial or is settled, often it is the degree of injury—rather than whether any actual medical negligence occurred—that is the determining factor whether compensation is paid, according to a Harvard study.*

One of the most common types of medical malpractice claims involving inadequate follow through occurs when prescribed medication is never actually administered. Typically, a physician prescribes a medication by writing an order in the physician portion or orders portion of a patient's chart. A nurse is then responsible for reading those records and accomplishing—or verifying the completion of—whatever the physician ordered. Most hospitals and medical facilities establish protocols whereby nurses "write off" medications ordered by physicians, verifying in the medical records that the prescribed medications have indeed been administered; once the nurse administers the medication he makes a note of such in the nurses notes and/or medications notes. However, physicians do not routinely read nurses notes (although my years as a medical malpractice defense attorney lead me to believe that, if at all possible, physicians should read nurses notes), and therefore on most occasions merely assume the medication they ordered was in fact timely administered. That physician would never know that a medication he ordered was not properly administered unless he in fact took the time to read through the nurses notes and/or medications notes. If the nurse responsible for administering the medication does not accomplish the task, hospitals and medical facilities typically have no safeguard in place to verify that the medication was in fact administered.

Some medical facilities have installed Computer Physician Order Entry systems ("CPOEs") in an effort to reduce prescription errors, as adverse drug events affect at least five percent (5%) of hospitalized patients, and another five to ten percent (5%-10%) of hospitalized patients experience potential adverse drug events, according to recent studies. However, less than five percent (<5%) of American hospitals utilize functioning CPOEs. Whether your facility has a CPOE, or whether you believe in the accuracy and effectiveness of such systems, the potential for human error—and computer error—obviously still exists, and you must employ your best efforts to avoid a malpractice claim based on a medication error that could have easily been prevented.

Real World Numbers: The Institute of Medicine reports that approximately one and a half million patients are injured each year by medication errors. A study published in 2006 in the Journal of the American Medical Association concluded that 2.5% of emergency room visits were due to adverse drug events, while 6.7% of hospitalizations for unintentional injuries were due to adverse drug events. Patients age 65 or older accounted for more than 25% of adverse drug event ER visits and 48.9% of adverse drug events requiring hospitalization.

Similarly, another frequent allegation of medical negligence regarding inadequate follow through involves tests, procedures, laboratory values and radiographic studies that are time sensitive. I have defended countless medical malpractice claims wherein a test or study was ordered by a physician "STAT" (by writing such in the chart), yet the test or study was not performed for hours or even days despite all health care providers involved in the case testifying under oath that STAT means "immediately," "right away," or at the very least "as soon as possible." Physicians consistently write in the medical records that they want something accomplished STAT, and then move on to the next patient, merely assuming the nurse, laboratory assistant, technician or other health care provider will accomplish the task. Hospitals, medical facilities and health care providers need to review, seriously and diligently, whatever protocols are in place regarding the ordering of time sensitive tests, labs, studies, etc. A prudent recommendation would be to establish protocols whereby the term STAT is uniformly utilized to represent one particular time demand, and "ASAP" or some other designation utilized to refer to a somewhat less urgent time demand. Plaintiffs lawyers enjoy a literal field day with the term STAT, and all health care providers should be aware of that fact.

One of the most frustrating situations I encounter as a defense attorney is defending a medical malpractice claim involving a diagnostic study, laboratory test or radiographic study ordered for a hospitalized patient—the results of which are to determine if the patient can be discharged—that is then not performed prior to that patient's discharge. If there is any cognizable injury whatsoever, a subsequent medical malpractice claim is extremely difficult to defend when the physician who orders a test or study be performed prior to discharge allows the patient to be discharged prior to completion of the test and interpretation of its results. Fortunately, in my practice, such has not been a frequent occurrence; but health care providers must absolutely ensure a patient is not discharged from the hospital or released from the ER before ordered tests are performed, and their results interpreted, noted in the chart and reviewed by the ordering or attending physician.

Real World Numbers: *A Harvard study of closed malpractice cases concluded that 59% involved diagnostic errors that harmed patients, the most common of which were failure to order appropriate tests (55%), failure to create a proper follow-up plan (45%) and failure to obtain a proper history or perform an adequate physical examination (42%). The leading factors contributing to these errors were physician failures in judgment (79%) and physician vigilance/memory (59%).*

Most health care facilities have established, written protocols regarding nearly every medical situation that may arise. Whether you are an employee of the facility or merely have privileges there, it is imperative you know the protocols of that facility, and not only from a quality of care standpoint. As previously discussed, a valid medical malpractice claim involves a breach of the standard of care, such standard of care being established by the health care providers in a given community or practice area (and, in malpractice claims/lawsuits, testified to by an expert witness). However, malpractice juries have also rendered verdicts of "liable" and awarded damages against health care providers who violate the procedures and protocols of the health care facility in which they practice, and there is nothing to stop juries from doing so in the future.

Plaintiffs lawyers lick their chops when their clients suffer an injury in a case where a physician with privileges at a hospital violates one of the hospital protocols, whether such violation actually contributes to the injury, or whether such violation is in fact a deviation of the applicable standard of care. A plaintiffs lawyer will utilize the physician's violation of the protocol as evidence the physician does not practice sound, quality medicine, arguing the physician is either unaware of the protocols of the facility where he has privileges or disregarded such protocols. In addition to practicing medicine within the standard of care, you must also know the procedures and protocols of the facilities where you practice and follow them, or risk being confronted regarding a violation of those protocols.

Real World Suggestions:

•   *consider enacting protocols whereby the administration of medications and other tasks to be accomplished by nurses or staff are periodically verified by a nurse supervisor, physician assistant or some other health care provider, or, devise a similarly thorough procedure whereby ordered tasks are verified as completed*

•   *enact office and/or facility procedures to ensure proper and timely follow through regarding external communication between physician and patient, especially regarding communication of test results* and time sensitive medical recommendations; if office or medical personnel are making follow-up phone calls regarding these communications, document such attempts and ensure multiple attempts are in fact made (leaving a voicemail message is not adequate, and follow through should not be considered complete until someone speaks with the patient or her legal guardian); unfortunately there is no hard and fast rule how many communication attempts health care providers must make, but in general if you try each type of communication three times you will demonstrate you made multiple attempts

- establish a uniform terminology for requested testing and procedures such that all medical personnel within the office or facility are aware that, for example, "STAT" means "within the next four hours," "ASAP" means "within the next twelve hours," etc.; if testing is to be performed outside the facility, ensure subsequent health care providers know what the abbreviation means, or, simply write out the complete request

- when communicating with patients outside an office or facility setting, consider utilizing a form of follow-up communication that can be ˙verified, such as certified or registered mail, computer e-mail—which can be verified as received and opened on a specific date and time— or some form of instant messaging; as technology evolves, consider utilizing new avenues to ensure and verify proper follow through, if prudent and effective

- only under specific circumstances should a physician consider writing a prescription for a patient he has never seen or examined; consider limiting the occasions you renew a prescription, or prescribe a new medication, without seeing the patient; if prescribing medication over the telephone for an established patient, ensure you properly document the occasion just as you would an office visit, including your medical judgment and reasons for so doing; never use pre-signed prescription pads; utilize one prescription pad per prescription

- in a case somewhat similar to the Real World Example on page 78, a nineteen-year-old woman with no family history of cancer presented to an oncologist complaining of a small mass in her breast; the oncologist *ordered radiographic studies and performed a fine needle aspiration, resulting in a diagnosis of fibroadenoma; over the next year the young woman developed three more small breast masses, which the oncologist continued to biopsy and which were revealed as fibroadenomas; when, two years later, the young woman again complained of a breast mass, the oncologist recommended lumpectomy, a procedure the young woman resisted; when the young woman never returned for a follow-up, the oncologist later stated he assumed/hoped the new mass—which upon palpation and radiographic studies appeared to possess benign characteristics—was just another fibroadenoma; the oncologist did not attempt any follow-up with the patient, but nine months later, when the new mass had grown significantly, the young woman finally acceded to her gynecologist's recommendation of biopsy, which revealed a malignancy; the woman sued the oncologist, alleging failure to diagnose/delay in diagnosis; the oncologist admitted he should have done more to follow-up with the patient, and to more diligently attempt to convince her to undergo biopsy/lumpectomy; the case had to be settled, considering expert witness testimony that the delay in diagnosis turned a stage one (node negative) case into a stage four (node positive) case*

5

Make Sure They Sign on the Dotted Line
Informed Consent

Most of the fundamental ideas of science are essentially simple, and may, as a rule, be expressed in a language comprehensible to everyone.

—Albert Einstein

One of the most important medical records contained in the entire chart is the informed consent document. In most states, performing non-emergent medical procedures without an executed informed consent document may result in a health care provider being charged with and convicted of a felony—battery. Although few health care providers would ever consider their attempts to treat a patient as a crime, everyone working in the field of medicine must be made aware how important the informed consent document is when defending a medical malpractice claim.

As you know, however, informed consent is not simply a piece of paper. Your medical education and training taught you that informed consent is a *process*— discussion, questions and answers, followed by understanding, comprehension, decision and, ultimately, consent. The physician must ensure the patient gives *knowledgeable* consent, meaning the physician has explained to the patient all the pertinent information regarding the proposed treatment or procedure, has provided the patient the opportunity to ask questions and has answered those questions to the patient's satisfaction, has documented the informed consent process in the medical records, and has secured the patient's signature on a thorough informed consent document signifying the patient is giving her knowledgeable consent to the treatment or procedure. Although you the physician know far more than the patient, it is the patient's body and therefore the patient's right to choose or refuse a treatment or procedure, after you have thoroughly explained the facts, diagnosis, risks and benefits.

Real World Numbers: In medical malpractice lawsuits that proceed to trial under a theory of lack of informed consent, when a thorough, executed informed consent document exists, the health care provider or medical facility successfully defends the lawsuit 74% of the time.

Jurors deciding medical malpractice cases generally want to find reasons to side with the physician or health care provider, most likely because people want to believe their doctors are competent, professional and right nearly all the time. To do so, however, jurors must combat their natural tendency to identify with a patient or family member, despite the fact that, as previously noted, on average individual health care providers prevail in medical malpractice cases that progress all the way to trial. A thorough, signed informed consent document detailing the exact risk about which the patient is now in court alleging medical negligence provides jurors a major piece of evidence they are looking for to find you not negligent and decide the case in your favor. More importantly, however, a thorough, executed informed consent document will also make a plaintiffs lawyer think twice about filing a medical malpractice claim against you, depending on the specific circumstances of the case.

A thorough, executed informed consent document certainly should not be considered blanket immunity against claims of medical malpractice, as a breach of the standard of care resulting in injury can lead to a claim of medical negligence no matter how thorough an informed consent document reads. However, in those instances where a patient alleges a physician failed to properly inform her of a procedure's potential risks and complications, when the patient's own signature verifies the physician discussed such possible occurrences, the patient and her lawyer will have an uphill battle arguing lack of informed consent. Additionally, the jury may mistrust a plaintiff who alleges lack of informed consent despite a thorough informed consent document with the plaintiff's signature on it; eroding the plaintiff's credibility with the jury is a tremendous benefit to a defendant health care provider's chances of prevailing at trial.

Real World Example: *A patient presented to the ER complaining of fever and intense lower abdominal pain, which the ER physicians determined was caused by acute diverticulitis. Subsequent to an informed consent discussion with the attending surgeon, the patient consented to emergency laparoscopic surgery by first signing the hospital's informed consent document and then signing another informed consent document required by the attending surgeon, who was not an employee or agent of the hospital. The laparoscopic procedure was successful, but during the operation the attending surgeon and two surgical residents inadvertently severed the patient's vas deferens—which, in this patient, was not located where the vas deferens is typically located. The severing of the vas deferens resulted both in the patient's sterility and a chronic testicular infection.*

The patient sued both the hospital—legally responsible for the actions of the two surgical residents—and the attending surgeon, alleging medical negligence and lack of informed consent. At trial, the plaintiffs lawyer argued that not only was it negligent to sever the vas deferens, but the hospital's informed consent document did not reflect any mention of risk to the urinary tract or reproductive capability. However, the second informed consent document—which was more thorough and contained the handwritten notation, "risks include . . . urinary function . . . sterility . . . impotence"—showed that the attending surgeon had discussed tertiary risk to the urinary tract and reproductive capability. The jury returned a verdict of no liability against the attending surgeon yet found the hospital liable for the negligence of the two surgical residents, premised on the hospital's informed consent document not delineating the potential risk of damage to the urinary tract or reproductive tract.

Many health care providers rely solely and exclusively on the pre-printed, boilerplate language contained on numerous informed consent forms. Some physicians merely instruct nurses or physician assistants to discuss potential risks and obtain the patient's signature on the pre-printed informed consent document. Other physicians may conduct the informed consent discussion themselves but then exit the room and allow nurses or physician assistants to answer the patient's questions and witness the patient's signature. But if a medical malpractice lawsuit proceeds to trial, you will quickly learn the only things important to jurors regarding an informed consent document are what is handwritten or highlighted/underlined as specific risks or complications of that particular procedure—not the generic risks of infection, death, etc.—and whether in fact the physician was present for and conducted the informed consent discussion himself.

Jurors seem to rationalize—utilizing their common sense—that to adequately explain a procedure and the potential risks involved, and to allow a patient the opportunity to ask questions about the procedure and associated risks, the physician himself must conduct the entire informed consent discussion. If the procedure is not emergent and time allows, conducting the informed consent discussion in your office to provide a patient the opportunity to reflect and ask questions is even more advantageous to both you and the patient (as opposed to obtaining consent at the hospital/facility or, even worse, in a pre-op holding area just minutes before the procedure). A study—evaluating a twenty-four-year period—published in the *Journal of Bone and Joint Surgery* found that an orthpaedic surgeon's risk of incurring a medical malpractice claim increased when informed consent was obtained on the hospital ward or in a pre-operative area, compared with a significantly decreased risk of incurring a claim when both informed consent was obtained in an office setting by the attending surgeon and the informed consent discussion was documented in the surgeon's office notes.

No matter how busy your practice is, as a physician you should view the informed consent discussion as a vital component of patient communication and care, and require yourself (and any subordinate physicians/residents) to participate in and witness the informed consent process. If you are a nurse or physician assistant you should do your best to request a physician's involvement in the informed consent process, and only sign the document as a witness if you are certain the patient does in fact understand and comprehend the risks and potential complications of the treatment/procedure.

Real World Suggestions:

        • *explain things simply and plainly; most patients can comprehend rudimentary medical discussions if you keep it simple, and you greatly decrease the chances of future problems if the patient knows exactly what is going to happen and what to expect post-procedure (malpractice claims oftentimes originate from a "surprise" negative outcome, but a patient who understands the bad result as "the risk the doctor warned me about" is less likely to file a claim than a patient "shocked" by a negative outcome)*

- *ensure you discuss patient expectations, perhaps even questioning the patient what exactly she expects as a result, both in an office setting and prior to the procedure; going over everything again provides a second opportunity for clarity and perhaps even a failsafe to ensure what you expect and what the patient expects are the same (additionally, conducting this discussion as part of the informed consent allows for more thorough confirmation in the medical records and for a witness to be present); remember, "Some people think that doctors and nurses can put scrambled eggs back into the shell," so ensure your patient's expectations are realistically aligned with your treatment goals so the patient will not be unduly disappointed*

- *never make any statements guaranteeing success, and consider documenting in the informed consent that the patient understands and acknowledges there is no guarantee of success*

- *provide the patient any educational materials you have regarding the disease, condition, treatment, etc., and note such in the chart; consider underlining, highlighting or starring any phrases in the materials you believe particularly relevant (this demonstrates to a plaintiffs lawyer or jury you not only provided the educational materials, but you went over them with the patient, too); always maintain generous supplies of educational materials so you are encouraged to disseminate them freely*

- *the greater a procedure's risk to a patient, the more carefully, slowly and thoroughly you should explain things to the patient; don't shortchange any informed consent process, but be especially diligent with potential problem cases or problem patients, perhaps even requesting permission for a family member to participate in the informed consent process*

- *even if your state or jurisdiction does not require a witness be present for the informed consent discussion, ensure a witness (i.e., nurse, physician assistant, etc.) is in fact present and signs the document as witnessing the informed consent discussion*

• *ensure you include whatever risks and potential complications are specific to the procedure you are performing, instead of merely relying on the language included on a pre-printed form; highlight any language on the pre-printed portion of the form if you consider it particularly relevant (e.g., circle "sterility" on the pre-printed portion of the form if the procedure you are performing carries an increased risk of sterility)*

• *if, due to her individual medical history or condition, a patient has an increased risk of some type of complication, discuss that risk thoroughly with the patient and note any increased risks/complications on the informed consent document and in your office notes/chart*

• *if possible, conduct the informed consent discussion in an office setting prior to the scheduled date of the procedure; document the discussion and patient's consent in your office notes/chart, being as specific as possible in both your notes and on the consent documents themselves*

• *for emergent cases or where the patient or guardian is unable/unavailable to give informed consent, do everything you can to save and/or care for the patient while appropriately documenting the inability to obtain proper informed consent; document your intention to obtain proper informed consent as soon as reasonably possible*

When faced with a medical malpractice insurance crisis in the 1980s, the American Society of Anesthesiologists ("ASA") initiated a project to determine what type of claims were being filed against anesthesiologists and how best to prevent them. After analyzing more than four thousand claims, the ASA found that one-third of claims were generated from adverse respiratory events, which are potentially the most damaging to patients yet the most preventable of all anesthesiology claims. In response, the ASA promoted the development and use of improved equipment and revised practice procedures, resulting both in improved care (fewer than four deaths per one million patient exposures) and decreased malpractice premiums (as of 2002, average anesthesiology premiums were at approximately the same level as they were in 1985).

6

Don't Hang Yourself
Admissions Against Interest

He is the best physician who is the most ingenuous inspirer of hope.
—Samuel Taylor Coleridge

In criminal law, it is the constitutional right not to incriminate oneself, memorialized in movies and on television by a lone witness on the stand passionately asserting, "I invoke my Fifth Amendment right against self-incrimination," or, "I plead the Fifth." It may not be quite so glamorous when standing in a hospital room next to a patient and her family, but the effect can be quite the same: depending what you say, how you say it, when you say it and to whom you say it, you may very well be setting up a slam-dunk medical malpractice claim by incriminating yourself with your own words.

As explained in Chapter B, medical malpractice lawsuits are civil proceedings, not criminal trials with the potential for incarceration. However, you may feel as if you want to hide in a prison cell if the seemingly innocuous statements you made to a patient or her family years ago eventually result in a multi-million dollar jury award against you.

Real World Numbers: *A hospital study concluded that failure to diagnose, and unexpected deaths in low risk hospitalizations, accounted for nearly 75% of all hospital mortalities attributable to adverse medical incidents. Decubitus ulcers, post-operative pulmonary embolism/deep-vein thrombosis, and post-operative respiratory failure accounted for almost 25% of hospital mortalities attributable to adverse medical incidents.*

Medical malpractice defense attorneys typically use the term "admission against interest" or "statement against interest," but what they are really referencing is self-incrimination in the civil sense. Anything a health care provider says that can be interpreted as admitting medical negligence—either on his own behalf or that of another health care provider—would be legally defined as an admission against interest because the health care provider is admitting someone did something wrong. When a police officer pulls you over when you know full well you were speeding, he typically asks, "Do you know why I pulled you over?" He is simply trying to get you to respond by admitting your guilt with some phrase that acknowledges you know you were speeding. And once you have said something like, "But Officer, I was just traveling with traffic and only going five miles over the limit," you have just admitted your guilt and the officer will note such to the judge if you attend traffic court to fight the citation. That is self-incrimination, and why *Miranda* rights advise you to remain silent because whatever you say can and will be used against you.

Your patient (or her family) will most likely not attempt to trick you into admitting you did something wrong that resulted in injury to the patient, but anything you say certainly can be used against you in a subsequent medical malpractice claim, and should a lawsuit be filed and the case proceed to trial, you definitely will hear your own words again: "Mrs. Smith, I feel terrible this happened during your surgery; I'm so sorry we (I, the attending, the resident, the surgeon, the anesthesiologist, the nurses, etc.) made a mistake that resulted in your injury." As honest, caring, warm and understanding as such a statement may sound, it also may affect whether a plaintiffs lawyer decides to take that patient's case, and perhaps even influence the outcome of any subsequent medical malpractice trial. Imagine a patient sitting in a plaintiffs lawyer's office saying, "And Dr. Jones admitted he did something wrong and apologized for hurting me." That plaintiffs lawyer's ears prick up and the wheels start turning; now he knows he's got a case he can sink his teeth into, one where the doctor may have admitted committing medical negligence. And think about those jurors listening intently while the plaintiffs lawyer gives his closing argument: "And ladies and gentlemen of the jury, why would Dr. Jones admit he committed malpractice and apologize for it if he didn't do anything wrong. Today, in this courtroom, when he's scared of losing his money and ruining his reputation, he's sitting here telling you he didn't do anything wrong; but two years ago when it was just him and the Smiths in that hospital room, he was honest with them, he felt bad for the mistake he made, and he told them he was sorry for his medical error."

You may now be asking yourself if you've just read an inconsistent statement, if you're getting conflicting suggestions, because on one hand you read in Chapter 1 about open, honest communication with your patients, but now you read about refraining from admitting just about anything. There is a definite line between precluding a medical malpractice claim because you are empathetic, understanding, explanatory and frank in your patient discussions, and, to the converse, contributing to a potential claim because you said too much. In most states/jurisdictions, you absolutely must stop short of admitting negligence, of saying that you or some other health care provider committed malpractice, that whatever happened to the patient was a result of a medical mistake.

Talk to your patient, but don't concede the lawsuit; you can accomplish the former without committing the latter.

The Medical Apology

Physicians may agree or disagree with offering a "medical apology" to the patient or family subsequent to an adverse medical incident, but some medical centers, health care institutions and malpractice insurers firmly believe in and practice the medical apology. You should be aware what a medical apology is, and whether you are even allowed to conduct a medical apology within your jurisdiction.

As discussed in Chapter 1, how you handle patient communications following a negative outcome or adverse medical incident may very well be the difference between facing a medical malpractice lawsuit and no claim ever being filed. A study published in the Journal of the American Medical Association *concluded that health care professionals were not providing the information and emotional support patients needed subsequent to committing medical mistakes that harmed patients, and that health care professionals should attempt to address a patient's desire for an explanation and, if warranted, an apology.*

Subsequent to any questionable event, you should consider doing all you can to be open, honest, communicative and understanding while making yourself fully available to the patient and/or her family (a physician providing the patient/family his cellular or home telephone number, despite the potential inconvenience, has prevented more than one malpractice claim). However, despite the obvious benefits of such frank, honest communication, an actual medical apology is a delicate event that should not be undertaken without full knowledge of the intricacies, ramifications and exact language that should be utilized. As previously discussed, every state has different laws regarding medical malpractice and a medical apology, and what is perfectly acceptable in Colorado might be an admission against interest and thus evidence of medical malpractice in Florida. You must verify what you can and cannot say, before you say it.

In general, most apologies consists of four components—acknowledgement, explanation, remorse and reparation. The acknowledgement should include details of the event, the persons involved and the unacceptable nature of the behavior. The explanation is the exact reasons for the event, although stating there is no explanation yet (e.g., "We're still trying to determine exactly what happened") is acceptable. Remorse is, of course, the genuine expression of contrition; if the expression is false or simply a pretense, the listener will sense it and the apology fail, doing more harm than good. Reparation is an attempt to make things right, even in a small way.

"Unfortunately, Mrs. Smith, a complication occurred during your husband's surgery when a nurse miscounted the number of sponges. I ended up leaving that uncounted sponge inside your husband, which caused an infection we couldn't stop. I am so terribly sorry this happened, and Nurse Jones is absolutely devastated. I know it's no consolation to you at this point, but we're going to implement new procedures to ensure something like this never happens again, and we certainly will not be billing you for the surgery or anything else. There is no way I can adequately convey to you how horrible I feel about this. I am so sorry—we're all so sorry."

Of course, any such conversation should occur with a nurse or other witness present, and should be conducted by the treating physician or appropriate specialist most involved in the care. In some states this medical apology is perfectly acceptable; in others, it's an admission against interest and evidence of malpractice. Your medical malpractice insurer or risk management department may conduct seminars detailing and explaining—for your particular state—a proper medical apology that not only succeeds in consoling the patient and/or her family while offering the desired explanation/closure, but also may help avoid a malpractice claim. Or, consult Appendix A and Appendix C for resources regarding conducting a proper medical apology within your state (or contact one of the local defense attorneys listed in Appendix D). Do not exacerbate an adverse medical incident resulting in injury to or death of a patient by conducting a medical apology that not only fails to appease/console the patient/family but provides a plaintiffs lawyer all the evidence he needs to sue you for malpractice. [Whether or not you believe in the effectiveness of medical apologies preventing malpractice claims—or whether you would even consider making a medical apology—you should know what you can and cannot say in your state to prevent making an admission against interest, even if you're not attempting to apologize.]

As of this book's printing, twenty-four state legislatures (Arizona, Colorado, Connecticut, Delaware, Georgia, Idaho, Illinois, Louisiana, Maine, Maryland, Missouri, Montana, New Hampshire, North Carolina, Ohio, Oklahoma, Oregon, South Dakota, Utah, Vermont, Virginia, Washington, West Virginia and Wyoming) have attempted to protect a health care provider's "apology" from ever being used against him in a medical malpractice claim/lawsuit by proposing or enacting laws that declare such apologies inadmissible in any claim, lawsuit or malpractice action. Some proposed/enacted laws protect statements of sympathy (e.g., "I'm sorry you suffered an injury") but not admissions of fault (e.g., "I'm sorry I caused you injury"). Every state and jurisdiction is different, the laws of which can change relatively quickly; discuss with a defense attorney, malpractice insurance professional, risk manager, hospital administrator or medical supervisor what you can and cannot say in your particular state, or consult the appendices.

Real World Example: *An elderly patient presented to the hospital for major abdominal surgery, performed by an attending physician and a surgical resident. The procedure was successful and, after seeing the still-hospitalized patient on the first post-operative day and noting recovery was progressing normally, the attending physician proceeded with his planned vacation. On the second and third post-op days the nurses observed a gradual deterioration of the patient's condition, noting such in the nurse's notes and verbally alerting the rounding surgical resident and attending physician on duty. When, on the fourth post-op day the patient continued to* *deteriorate, the surgical resident finally telephoned the vacationing attending, who made some general inquiries but otherwise did not contribute anything more to the patient's care. On the sixth post-op day the patient "crashed," and expired the following day. The attending physician returned home from vacation and met with the patient's family, who inquired why the patient deteriorated so severely post-op, why the patient died.*

The attending physician apologized to the family, and said, "This never should have happened. It's my fault for not returning early to take care of her, and for not insuring she was in good hands when I left. This was a mistake that could have and should have been avoided." The attending physician later told me he merely said these things to appease and comfort the family even though he did not believe he or any other health care provider committed malpractice, but in the resulting medical malpractice lawsuit the attending physician, resident, on duty attending, nurses and hospital were all forced to settle the case. The attending physician's statements implicated not only himself, but the entire medical team caring for the patient; based on the attending physician's statements, every health care provider involved in the patient's care was held legally responsible in some way. [This was a Florida case, where a physician's apologetic statements are considered an admission against interest and thus can be utilized as evidence of malpractice. As of this book's printing, such was still Florida law.]

To the legal system, to lawyers, words are the stock in trade. Whether they are contained within the medical records or spoken aloud, words make or break a medical malpractice case. And when a patient and her family tell a plaintiffs lawyer, or jurors in a medical malpractice trial, that a health care provider admitted committing malpractice and apologized for making a medical error, that plaintiffs lawyer begins to salivate, those medical malpractice jurors begin to compute the amount of damages they are going to award the patient. Choosing your words carefully may never be as important.

Real World Suggestions:

- *consider immediately—prior to any adverse medical incident occurring—discussing with your malpractice insurer, attorney, medical facility or supervisor (and with your medical colleagues) your potential approach to patient discussions subsequent to a negative outcome or adverse medical incident to determine—or reaffirm—whether you will in fact conduct explanatory (or apologetic) patient discussions and to what extent*

- *when discussing why a particular outcome was not achieved or why a negative result occurred, avoid assigning blame to anyone while trying to explain what happened*

- *avoid using the word "fault" during any patient discussion (including when the patient may be at fault, such as not ceasing smoking prior to a surgical procedure or not informing you of pertinent medical history)*

- *although you may believe another health care provider committed negligence or provided inappropriate care, avoid criticizing any other health care provider, just as you would not want another health care provider to criticize your care and treatment (even if that health care provider is your nurse, your superior, your partner or your colleague; in general, as "captain of the ship," a physician is typically held legally responsible for the negligent acts of his nurses, employees, etc.); you may not know all the facts surrounding another health care provider's treatment, you may not practice the same specialty or discipline, you may not have access to all previous and subsequent medical records, and you certainly do not want to be forced to act as an expert witness for the plaintiffs lawyer against another health care provider*

- *in cases where you believe you provided appropriate care, express sympathy for a negative outcome (e.g., "I'm so sorry for your loss") but do not apologize for your actions/care*

- *some studies show that patients often file malpractice claims in part because they are angry about a medical bill charging them for what they believe was* negligent medical care (such patients perceive it as not receiving value for their money); so, if you suspect a patient is contemplating a malpractice claim, consider not seeking payment for the medical services you rendered regarding the treatment in question, but first verify with a defense attorney in your state (or your malpractice insurer or risk management department) whether waiving a medical bill serves as a tacit admission of wrongdoing

- prior to any medical apology or explanatory communication, meet with all involved medical personnel to establish the known medical facts to assist in providing an accurate explanation; document any such meetings (remember, in general, any such meetings and the information discussed therein are "privileged" (confidential) and protected from disclosure in a medical malpractice claim or lawsuit)

- consider contacting a defense attorney, risk manager, facility administrator, hospital supervisor or medical superior prior to any discussions with the patient or her family regarding an adverse medical incident

- when contemplating a discussion with a patient or her family subsequent to an adverse medical incident, develop a plan ahead of time—what to say and how to say it, choosing your words carefully; don't wing it or speak off the cuff

- when conducting an explanatory discussion or medical apology with a patient or family member, always ensure a nurse or other witness is present (so years later a medical malpractice case doesn't boil down to "he said, she said")

- consider attending a medical apology lecture or seminar prior to being faced with an adverse medical incident requiring a medical apology, so that you are adequately prepared in advance

- even if your state does not allow medical apologies, or if you do not believe in medical apologies and thus are certain you will never make one, arm yourself with the requisite knowledge to avoid making an admission against interest or otherwise damaging your defense in a medical malpractice lawsuit

Nearly one out of every twenty-five patients in America with myocardial infarctions (approximately 12,000 people a year) are mistakenly sent home from an emergency room, hospital or medical facility.

7

Dance With Who Brought You
Practice Areas

The best doctor is the veterinarian. He can't ask his patients what is the matter—he's got to just know.
—Will Rogers

Physicians and other health care providers get themselves into trouble—big trouble—when they try to do something they're simply not trained to do. The medical profession, and most reasonable medical malpractice juries, recognizes there is always a first time, a first patient, a first procedure. But what the legal profession seeks to prevent in the medical profession is an untrained, inexperienced health care provider attempting alone to render care in a practice area in which he simply has no business providing care: the orthopaedist venturing into complex neurosurgery, the family practitioner diagnosing a rare infectious disease he has never previously seen, the pediatrician attempting a skin graft. And, even if a procedure is within a physician's practice area, if that physician has never performed the procedure, he is opening himself up to serious liability if, at a minimum, he does not seek the assistance of a physician skilled and experienced in that procedure.

If you are trained in a particular specialty, stick with that specialty, at least until you receive additional education, training and experience; there is no substitute for formal training programs and refresher courses for procedures rarely performed. Although *see one, do one, teach one* has long been a mantra of medical education, perhaps *see five, assist five, do five, teach one* would be more appropriate phraseology in today's world, at least from a medical malpractice defense standpoint. Observing procedures performed outside your specialty by trained, experienced practitioners and then progressively becoming more and more involved in those procedures under proper supervision will almost certainly provide you the requisite background to become proficient in other practice areas, but for purposes of suggestions how to reduce the risks of being sued for malpractice, such definitely provides a further layer of legal defense.

Just as at one time you were a medical student and then a resident, observing and then slowly participating in procedures, so too must you slowly and patiently delve into a different practice area, or into new or advanced procedures, despite the fact you are a fully qualified physician in your specific practice area. Consider viewing yourself as an intern or second-year resident when interested in a new procedure or practice area, requiring yourself to undergo the same training and experience before performing any new or different procedures/diagnoses. Just because you know how to perform an open abdominal procedure does not mean you know how to perform a laparoscopic abdominal procedure. If you think you need help with a diagnosis or encounter something you simply can't explain, ask for assistance, another mind to work on the problem, the benefit of another physician's education, knowledge, background and experiences. A health care provider practicing outside his field or expertise is a prime and easy target for the medical malpractice plaintiffs lawyer, and jurors will definitely want to know what qualifications and experience you have to do so.

Real World Example: A patient with a history of priapism presented to a urologic surgeon complaining of pain subsequent to a sexual encounter which left his penis bent at an angle. Based on his reading medical journal articles regarding a new procedure to alleviate the effects of priapism, the urologic surgeon recommended surgery to relieve the pain by treating the priapism, a condition from which the patient suffered for over twenty years and which the patient and his wife stated they did not mind one bit.

The patient consented to the procedure, which the urologic surgeon had never previously performed; the urologic surgeon failed to advise the patient of this fact. The urologic surgeon did not consult any other urologists or physicians prior to performing the surgery. Subsequent to the procedure, the patient's priapism—and pain—resolved, but due to misplacement of surgical sponges by the urologic surgeon the patient was rendered permanently impotent. The patient and his wife sued the urologic surgeon for malpractice, based on the urologic surgeon's inexperience in performing the procedure. Considered an indefensible case if it proceeded to trial, the lawsuit was settled shortly after being filed.

Even within your specialty you must remain vigilant, must always seek to improve your knowledge, education and practice. Believe it or not, numerous studies have found decreasing physician performance with increasing years in practice. In fact, a recent review published in the *Annals of Internal Medicine* found that, for patients suffering heart attacks, mortality increased 0.5% for every year the treating physician had been out of medical school; and only 4% of the review's studies found increased physician performance with increased physician age. The farther removed a physician from medical school and residency, the less of a sense he may have of the improving standards of care, of new technologies, treatment modalities, procedures. We all tend to identify a comfort level with our education, knowledge and experience and oftentimes find ourselves practicing our professions solely within that sphere (I constantly remind myself to try to learn something new from attorneys fresh out of law school or transferring in from a different practice environment). You know your practice better than anyone, so you know how best to improve it; do all you can to educate, train, and refresh yourself, by whatever means available.

Real World Numbers: *Eighty percent (80%) of all medical malpractice claims filed in the United States involve allegations of negligence in one of four areas: medication errors, missed/delayed diagnosis, obstetrics or surgery.*

The converse, however, may be equally true. Physicians fresh out of residency—and health care providers right out of school, training or clinical programs— may hold an edge in the latest standards of care, but fragmentation of care as a result of the recent "shift" mentality of medical practice may create more opportunities for the occurrence of adverse medical incidents. A 2006 study published in the *American Journal of Medicine* found that as residents' hours have been reduced and restricted, both attendings and residents fear a lack of continuity of patient care may result in increased adverse medical incidents. Residents also expressed they were not learning as much or as fast as they should, and worried it might negatively impact patient care. Attendings reported fearing residents were becoming mere "shift workers" and not learning to view the patient as *their* patient, not assuming the role of their patient's advocate and champion, not taking responsibility for the overall well-being of their charge but instead simply performing tasks on the facility's patients while they were on duty. A study conducted at Brigham and Women's Hospital in Boston found that hospital complications and medical errors occurred more frequently at night, when patients were being cared for by different physicians personally unfamiliar with the patients and their conditions.

> *Real World Numbers:* A study published in the Annals of Internal Medicine in 2006 concluded that in malpractice cases involving diagnostic errors that harmed patients, "handoffs" contributed to physician errors 20% of the time.

In an effort to teach younger physicians to be more empathetic with their patients and instill a sense of "patient ownership," Harvard, the University of Pennsylvania and a number of other medical schools have implemented pilot programs wherein students are paired with patients to "shadow" them through the health care system as the patients set about the often confusing and laborious task of seeking and receiving medical care for their illnesses/conditions. These programs attempt to teach physicians to view each patient as a complex combination of both illness and health ranging across multiple biological systems, and to understand that treating the patient as a whole individual across all fields and not simply as a series of symptoms benefits both the patient receiving the care and the physician administering it by improving the overall quality of care rendered and received. Physicians report that learning to view both patient health and the health care system from the patient's perspective assists patient and health care provider achieve the desired result from the medical system. Physicians farther removed from residency may have to constantly refresh their education and knowledge base to improve the level of care they provide, but physicians less removed from residency must attempt to adopt a more engaged and invested approach to total patient care.

In addition to remaining vigilant regarding new developments, technologies and standards of care, health care providers must also remain vigilant in their approach to diagnosis and treatment. I have defended numerous cases in which a patient's complaints were continually and repeatedly met by the exact same ineffectual treatment modality, as the health care provider did nothing to approach the complaints with an alternate treatment modality or consider another etiology or differential diagnosis. As a physician, you must persevere in or adopt an open-minded approach to addressing patient's symptoms in the face of repeated failures of known treatment modalities or etiologies, if not from a medical perspective then from a legal defense standpoint.

Real World Example: *An orthopaedic surgeon who treated both college and professional athletes was supervising the rehabilitation of an athlete's broken leg. The athlete complained of pain, tightness and cramping in the leg, which, upon examination and palpation of a "bump," the orthopaedic surgeon attributed to a muscle cramp or "charley horse." The athlete continued to complain of the same symptoms, and after nearly four months the orthopaedic surgeon finally ordered radiographic studies, which revealed a mass in the leg; subsequent to biopsy, the mass was determined malignant. The athlete filed a medical malpractice claim against the orthopedic surgeon, alleging failure to diagnose/delay in diagnosis of the malignant mass. The orthopaedic surgeon confessed he assumed the complaints were related to the broken leg and that he never considered another diagnosis.*

The above example demonstrates that health care providers must be proactive, must consider other etiologies on the differential diagnosis spectrum, must consider approaching complaints in an alternate manner when prior treatments do not work. When the facts of a case do not fit a particular diagnosis, physicians must explore other possibilities, must think outside the box. A young athlete may not be a prime candidate for presence of a malignant mass of the leg (and, as discussed on page 83, a woman in her early twenties, with no family history of cancer but a documented history of benign fibroadenomas, may not be a prime candidate for a malignant breast mass), but when a physician palpates a mass, tumor should at least be on the differential diagnosis and aggressively explored, especially when no other etiology is found. Whether a health care provider far removed from formal education and training or a relatively fresh face still learning the ropes, you must remain open to new or rare diagnoses of complaints/symptoms that may not immediately fit a common explanation, always practicing within the prevailing standard of care.

Real World Suggestions:

- *practice only within your field, where you are educated, trained and experienced*
- *consult specialists and health care providers in other fields when you choose to enter other practice areas; take appropriate classes, seminars, courses, etc. within those fields and be able to provide documentation of successful completion*
- *continue to educate yourself and keep current within your field; take courses, attend seminars, subscribe to medical journals and read them religiously; consider rounding/consulting with physicians within your practice area who are less removed from residency than you*
- *less experienced practitioners should consider focusing on continuity of care and viewing such care as a continuum, not the fragmented, task-oriented approach "shift" medical care is perhaps becoming*
- *don't blindly follow orders if you have a legitimate, well-founded concern; question something you feel simply does not make sense, and if the response is not satisfactory, consider asking a supervisor or additional medical personnel (you not only may prevent yourself and other health care providers from being sued, you may even improve patient care)*
- *consider differential diagnoses and alternative treatment modalities, especially when the treatment course you've chosen is not working; consult liberally with other health care providers when you question the efficacy of a treatment course*

A study published in 2006 in the *Annals of Internal Medicine* concluded that fundamental physician error— not timely ordering tests, failure to order tests and failure to follow through—was involved in almost 60% of cases in which patients alleged injury due to missed or delayed diagnosis. Of the cases studied, 30% resulted in death.

Afterword, But Not Afterthoughts
Rendering Appropriate Care
Peer Disclosure of Medical Errors
Your Medical Malpractice Insurance Policy

Men who are occupied in the restoration of health . . . are above all the great of the earth.   They even partake of divinity, since to preserve and renew is almost as noble as to create.
—Voltaire

A study published in the *New England Journal of Medicine* found that, of the over 13,000 patients spread across twelve metropolitan areas who participated in the study, only 55% received the complete extent of medical care recommended by physicians.   Although there obviously are numerous factors why a patient might not receive recommended care, including factors outside a health care provider's control, that so many patients did not receive the care they should equates to a vast opportunity to increase the quality of medical care in the United States.   Physicians and other health care providers may not want to hear it, but simply improving the quality of care they provide would reduce the number of medical malpractice claims filed.

Real World Numbers: According to the National Practitioner Data Bank kept by the Department of Health and Human Services, from 1990 to 2002,

• 2,774 American physicians incurred five or more medical malpractice payouts (jury awards against them or settlements paid on their behalf), yet only one in six of these physicians were disciplined by a state medical board
• of the nearly 35,000 American physicians with two or more medical malpractice payouts, only eight percent (8%) were disciplined by state medical boards
• just five percent (5%) of all American physicians were responsible for fifty-four percent (54%) of all medical malpractice payouts
• one physician incurred 24 medical malpractice payouts from 1993 to 2001, totaling more than eight million dollars; he was never disciplined by medical authorities

---

Nearly every health care provider well knows that a 1999 Institute of Medicine study concluded that as many as 98,000 deaths result from medical errors every year in the United States, and that another 1,000,000 people are injured every year as a result of medical errors. A separate *HealthGrades* study published in 2004 found that, on average, 195,000 patients die each year from in-hospital medical errors. A 2006 *Time* magazine "Notebook" section, citing the Institute of Medicine, proclaimed, "1.5 million: Average number of patients injured a year by medication errors of health professionals, including doctors' bad handwriting" and "$3.5 billion: Annual cost of treating those drug-related injuries." Plastered across the advertisements and websites of plaintiffs lawyers throughout the country are phrases such as, "The United States loses more

American lives to patient safety incidents every six months than it did in the entire Vietnam War," and, "Chances are you or someone you know has been a victim of medical malpractice." Simply put, the statistics are out there— whether medical professionals want to acknowledge them or debate their efficacy—and plaintiffs lawyers are using those statistics to educate potential plaintiffs, to bring legal business in the door, to file medical malpractice claims against you.

I certainly recommend you do all you can to follow the suggestions in this book in an effort to reduce the chances a patient will file a medical malpractice claim against you, but I hope you also find that utilizing some of these suggestions may improve the overall patient care you provide. As it is your practice, your career, your profession, you most likely know dozens of ways to improve the quality of care you render. Whether you implement an office protocol whereby an assistant periodically telephones diabetic patients to ensure they have completed at least three glycosylated hemoglobin tests over a two-year period and verify receipt of the results of those tests, create a mail or telephone reminder that elderly patients come in for their pneumococcal vaccine, institute a policy that unless contraindicated all myocardial infarction patients receive beta-blockers, or simply begin fully writing out a few commonly confused medical terms you previously abbreviated, you know best how to approach the task of attempting to somehow improve the quality of care you provide.

Whether you're a physician or nurse, dentist or psychologist, podiatrist or chiropractor, physician assistant or nurse anesthetist, phlebotomist or radiographic technician, I'm certain at this very moment, with your very next patient, you can think of at least three ways to improve the quality of medical care you provide, without sacrificing efficiency or compromising protocol. This book can't tell you how best to improve your own individual practice, your personal approach to patient care; you are the only one who can consider this book's suggestions and modify your practice accordingly, advancing overall patient care and further reducing the chances you'll be sued for medical malpractice.

Peer Disclosure of Medical Errors

As discussed in Chapter 1, health care providers may be hesitant to fully disclose medical errors to patients or their families for a variety of reasons, which may actually encourage patients to file medical malpractice claims as the only means to obtain the answers, apologies or closure they seek. Health care providers may also decline to disclose medical errors to their peers or superiors, which not only can affect a medical facility's ability to combat a potential medical malpractice claim but may also result in missed opportunities to improve future medical care. Oftentimes, physicians and health care providers are embarrassed or ashamed of committing a medical error and choose not to report the error for fear their peers or superiors will think them incompetent, "a bad doctor." However, sometimes the best way to learn is from mistakes, and disclosing and discussing a mistake is usually the best way to learn from it.

Morbidity and mortality conferences seek to encourage the disclosure of medical errors in a neutral setting—where the goal is improving patient safety rather than punishing a health care provider—as open discussion of medical errors may increase reporting of medical errors, as well as promote improved patient care. Physicians and other medical personnel should not hesitate to disclose and discuss medical errors during conferences/meetings, and should be encouraged to do so by peers and superiors. From a legal standpoint, any information disclosed or discussed in these peer review conferences is typically considered "privileged," meaning the law protects and precludes its disclosure to the plaintiffs lawyer, the jury or the public; in general, information disclosed and discussed during these conferences cannot be utilized in any way in a medical malpractice claim/lawsuit.

Full disclosure and discussion during conferences should be encouraged and fostered in every way possible, as health care providers must be made to feel comfortable discussing medical errors. A study published in the *Journal of the American Medical Association* concluded that in both surgery and internal medicine morbidity and mortality conferences, attending physicians missed opportunities during medical error discussions to model recognition of error and to employ specific examples by explaining their own personal medical error experiences. The study found that internal medicine conferences spent most of the time presenting cases and listening to invited speakers rather than discussing medical errors, and even when medical errors were mentioned they were less likely to be discussed as an actual error, or were ignored altogether. In both internal medicine and surgery conferences, when medical errors were actually discussed, only 40% were discussed explicitly. The study's findings contrasted with other studies of residency directors that reported 80% of the directors believed morbidity and mortality conferences adequately addressed unexpected adverse events/suspected errors and that they were fully discussed with a moderate to high degree of success.

Another study published in the *Journal of the American Medical Association* found that only 54% of residents informed their attending physicians about the most serious errors they made within the previous year (of the errors actually reported, 31% resulted in death); serious errors, especially, should be disclosed and discussed with the attending physicians directly and legally responsible for patient care. Residents and health care providers fresh from school or clinical training must be taught to recognize, acknowledge, disclose and discuss medical errors as one of the best means to improve patient care; a perhaps unintended but certainly tangible benefit is the reduction of medical malpractice claims.

A defense attorney writing a book about the prevention of medical malpractice claims may not have the medical credentials to suggest to health care providers they improve peer disclosure and discussion of medical errors, but if anything will reduce the chances of having a claim filed against you it is an overall improvement of medical care and patient safety. If, as numerous studies conclude, patient safety and the quality of medical care rendered can be improved by frank, open disclosure and discussion during peer conferences, then that is a goal not only health care providers and patients want, but defense attorneys, too.

Your Medical Malpractice Insurance Policy

Most physicians and health care providers cannot describe their medical malpractice insurance policies, other than what they pay in premiums, as many have never even read their policies. Some health care providers are covered by malpractice insurance through their employer or facility, but whether or not you are responsible for maintaining insurance for yourself, it is imperative you know what type of policy you have and what it covers. If you are uninsured, you should know the insurance coverages available to protect your assets.

A medical malpractice insurance policy contract consists of two parts—the policy form and the declarations sheet ("Dec. Page"). The policy form has five basic components: the Definitions section (where important terms are defined); the actual insuring agreement (which specifies the insurance company will pay—up to the liability limits— for any liability resulting from covered medical acts committed by the insured); the Conditions (which delineate the insured's and insurer's responsibilities, such as the insured promptly reporting claims, assisting in defending the case, etc.); Exclusions (acts not covered by the policy, such as practicing without a valid license, or practicing while impaired by drugs or alcohol); Miscellaneous. The second part, the Dec. Page, spells out the liability limits and amount of coverage, the persons covered by the policy, the policy period, the premium to be paid, and the type of coverage (occurrence or claims made).

An *occurrence* policy covers you only for incidents that occur while the insurance policy is in force, much like homeowners or automobile insurance. Even if you discontinue an occurrence policy, as long as you had coverage when the medical incident occurred, it does not matter when the claim is filed (in rare instances, claims can be filed decades after the original medical incident, but an occurrence policy still covers you in such cases). Occurrence policies typically cost more than claims made policies and are becoming increasingly rare.

A *claims made* policy covers a health care provider for claims reported while the policy is in force, even if the medical incident occurred prior to when you purchased the policy (most claims made policies require disclosure of known medical incidents occurring prior to the policy's effective date). However, two dates are important on a claims made policy—the retroactive date (the original coverage date for the insured by this particular insurer) and the reporting date of the claim. To be covered by a claims made policy, the medical incident must occur after the retroactive date and be reported during the policy period. For coverage regarding any medical incident that occurred prior to the retroactive date, if you do not have an occurrence policy to cover the period in which the incident occurred the only way that incident would be covered is if you purchased a *tail* policy/rider for your claims made policy or if you purchased *nose* coverage by backdating the retroactive date of the claims made policy. It is vital you are aware that under a claims made policy, if you allow such to lapse or you discontinue coverage you must obtain either tail coverage or nose coverage from any new insurer or there will be a gap in coverage and you will be exposed to personal liability. Malpractice insurance coverage can be quite confusing and it is highly recommended you seek professional assistance to ensure you are adequately covered and your assets appropriately protected.

Whether you have a claims made or occurrence policy, your insurer will pay the costs to defend you in any claim or lawsuit, and the defense costs will not reduce the liability limits available to pay claims (termed "outside the limits"). Occasionally, policies pay defense costs "inside the limits"—meaning the liability limits available to pay claims are reduced by the amount it costs to defend you—but such policies are still rare. If you are uninsured, you are responsible for paying your own defense costs. Although some health care providers maintain malpractice insurance through their employers, it is still essential you know what is contained within your policy. What is best for your employer in terms of coverage may not be best for you individually, and you should know how your departure from your employer affects you insurance-wise.

Malpractice insurance policies contain liability limits, and you should be aware that if a claim exceeds your policy limits you may be held personally responsible for the excess. You should consider maintaining liability limits that are standard for your geographic area or type of practice, but many health care providers maintain at least $1,000,000.00 in coverage per occurrence/medical incident, with a $3,000,000.00 maximum per year. However, some health care providers believe they appear a more attractive target for malpractice claims the more insurance coverage they carry and therefore maintain as little coverage as possible (including no coverage at all), hoping to dissuade potential lawsuits based on presenting themselves as financially not worth the effort. These health care providers typically rely on a knowledgeable asset protection professional to more fully insulate themselves from lawsuits. Whether you favor either extreme or find yourself somewhere in the middle, ensure you know how much coverage you have and what it includes.

An *umbrella* policy provides an extra layer of coverage in addition to either a claims made or occurrence policy. Umbrella policies are often inexpensive, and occasionally even free of charge, but their most important feature is they may cover any excess that occurs over and above your policy limits, thereby protecting your personal assets should a jury award or legal judgment exceed your policy limits. However, some health care providers simply prefer to increase their liability limits as opposed to procuring umbrella coverage, or obtain an *excess* policy. Verify with your employer or insurance carrier whether you have an umbrella policy, or if you can obtain one, and seek the assistance of insurance professionals to ensure you maintain adequate coverage. [As you can see from this brief summary, malpractice insurance is typically alien to anyone not in the insurance business, and you are strongly urged to contact an insurance professional if you have any questions. If you are uninsured or considering practicing without insurance, it is imperative you at least discuss with, if not retain, a professional asset manager to fully advise you and protect your assets.]

YOUR DEFENSE ATTORNEY
Who's On Your Side?

If the law supposes that . . . the law is an ass.
—Charles Dickens

Your medical malpractice insurer, the hospital where you practice or the health care facility in which you work most likely will provide you a defense attorney responsible for defending your care and representing your interests as your attorney. If you do not carry medical malpractice insurance and are not an employee of a hospital, health care system, medical facility or health care office, you may be responsible for retaining your own defense attorney (Appendix D will help you locate a local defense attorney should you need one). Nothing prevents you from hiring your own attorney regardless if one is provided you, but you would then be personally responsible for your attorney's fees and costs. When sued, many health care providers retain their own defense attorneys based on their desire to be represented by someone who has no other client or loyalty, despite the fact legal ethics rules stipulate that when a defense attorney is retained by a malpractice insurance company his true client is the health care provider himself.

Depending on your malpractice insurance policy or employer's protocols, you may also desire to retain your own attorney if you receive a "reservation of rights" letter from your or your employer's malpractice insurance carrier. You would receive such a letter in cases where the plaintiff alleges you committed acts not covered under the policy (e.g., fraud, sexual relations with a patient, etc.). The insurance company should continue to fully defend you in the case, but if the only allegations proven true are those not covered by the policy, the insurance company will seek reimbursement from you for the expenses it paid to defend you (and not pay any judgment entered against you). If you receive a reservation of rights letter, consider retaining an attorney to handle any dealings with the insurance company and/or to act as co-counsel or "shadow counsel" in defending against the malpractice claim.

In general, though, even if you don't personally like the defense attorney assigned by your malpractice insurer to defend you, he may in fact be the best person for the job, based on his training and experience. You certainly should be comfortable with your legal representation, but it is more important you have the right attorney for the task at hand. If, however, you feel that you absolutely cannot work with that defense attorney for the next few years, do not hesitate to request another attorney be assigned to represent you, or consider retaining your own attorney.

Real World Example: *A surgeon was sued for malpractice subsequent to leaving his former hospital to practice in another state, such lawsuit being filed in the physician's former state of residence regarding care he previously provided. His former hospital furnished him a defense attorney to represent him in the lawsuit, and the defense attorney flew across the country to meet the surgeon in the surgeon's new state of residence prior to the plaintiffs lawyer conducting the surgeon's deposition. The defense attorney's flight was unfortunately delayed, and a passenger on the flight spilled an entire glass of bourbon on him. The defense attorney arrived in the surgeon's new city of residence in the middle of a dawn blizzard, and the airline lost the attorney's luggage. The attorney was forced to sleep an hour or two at the airport before the blizzard cleared long enough for the attorney to* make it to the surgeon's office for the deposition, which the plaintiffs lawyer was conducting via telephone.

When the surgeon met the defense attorney—who reeked of bourbon, hadn't slept in two days and looked completely rumpled and disheveled in his dirty clothes—the surgeon immediately objected to the defense attorney representing him. The defense attorney suggested the surgeon contact the hospital to arrange alternate legal counsel, but as the deposition was scheduled for later that morning the defense attorney recommended the surgeon wait until after the deposition to request replacement counsel. The surgeon finally assented, and the defense attorney set about preparing the surgeon for his deposition. The deposition proceeded and went extremely well from the defense standpoint; the surgeon reconsidered his position, ultimately deciding not to request replacement counsel. The defense attorney successfully represented the surgeon throughout the lawsuit and trial.

Studies indicate surgical patients have a 31% greater chance of death when hospitalized in a facility where the typical nurse cares for more than seven patients. On average, for every additional patient a nurse cares for, patient mortality rises 7%.

ENDNOTES

14 When surveyed regarding: Baker T. *The medical malpractice myth.* Chicago: University of Chicago Press. 2005;95.

21 Real World Numbers: Forster HP, Schwartz J, DeRenzo E. Reducing legal risk by practicing patient-centered Medicine. *Arch Intern Med.* 2002;162:1217-1219.

23 a Harvard Study reported: Harvard Medical Practice Study. *Patients, doctors, and lawyers: Medical injury, malpractice litigation, and patient compensation in New York: The report of the Harvard Medical Practice Study to the State of New York.* Cambridge: Harvard University. 1990.

29 Numerous studies have attempted: Hickson GB, Clayton EW, Githens PB, Sloan FA. Factors that prompted families to file medical malpractice claims following perinatal injuries. *JAMA.* 1992;267:1359-1363; and, Forster HP, Schwartz J, DeRenzo E. Reducing legal risk by practicing patient-centered medicine. *Arch Intern Med.* 2002;162:1217-1219.

29 Real World Numbers: Forster HP, Schwartz J, DeRenzo E. Reducing legal risk by practicing patient-centered medicine. *Arch Intern Med.* 2002;162:1217-1219; and, Clinton HR, Obama B. Making patient safety the centerpiece of medical liability reform. *N Engl J Med.* 2006;354:2205-2208.

38   Real World Numbers: Clinton HR, Obama B. Making
      patient safety the centerpiece of medical liability reform.
      N Engl J Med. 2006;354:2205-2208.

40   One study found: Stelfox H, Ghandi T, Orav E,
      Gustafson M. The relation of patient satisfaction with
      complaints against physicians and malpractice lawsuits.
      Am J Med. 2005;10:1126-1133.

42   Real World Facts: Levinson W, Roter DL, Mullooly JP,
      Dull VT, Frankel RM. Physician-patient communication.
      The relationship with malpractice claims among primary
      care physicians and surgeons. *JAMA.* 1997;277:553-
      559; and, Hickson GB, Federspiel CF, Pichert JW, Miller
      CS, Gauld-Jaeger J, Bost P. Patient complaints and
      malpractice risk. *JAMA.* 2002;287:2951-2957.

43   Other studies indicate. Larsen KM, Smith CK.
      Assessment of non-verbal communication in the
      patient-physician interview. *Journal of Family Practice.*
      1981:12;481-488.

47   The average physicians interrupts: Marvel MK, Epstein
      RM, Flowers K, Beckham HB. Soliciting the patient
      agenda: Have we improved? *JAMA. 1999;281:283-287.*

56   Real World Numbers: Insurance Information Institute,
      2005.

59   Defensive Medicine: Studdert DM, Mello MM, Sage WM,
      DesRoches CM, Peugh J, Zapert K, Brennan TA.
      Defensive medicine among high-risk specialist
      physicians in a volatile malpractice environment.
      JAMA. 2005;293:2609-2617.

79   Real World Fact: Brennan TA, Sox CM, Burstin HR.
      Relation between negligent adverse events and the
      outcomes of medical malpractice litigation. *N Engl J
      Med.* 1996;335:1963-1967.

80   least five percent: Bates DW, Cullen DJ, Laird N.
      Incidence of adverse drug events and potential adverse

drug events: Implications for prevention: ADE Prevention Group Study. *JAMA.* 1995;274:29-34.

80   Real World Numbers: Budnitz DS, Pollock DA, Weidenbach KN, Mendelsohn AB, Schroeder TJ, Annest JL.   National surveillance of emergency department visits for outpatient adverse drug events. *JAMA.* 2006;296:1858-1866.

81   Real World Numbers: Gandhi TK, Kachalia A, Thomas EJ, Puopolo AL, Yoon C, Brennan TA, Studdert DM. Missed and delayed diagnosis in the ambulatory setting: A study of closed malpractice claims. *Ann Intern Med.* 2006;145;488-496.

86   Real World Numbers: Studdert DM, Mello MM, Gawande AA, Gandhi TK, Kachalia A, Yoon C, Puopolo AL, Brennan TA.   Claims, errors, and compensation payments in medical malpractice litigation. *N Engl J Med.* 2006;354:2024-2033.

89   A study—evaluating a twenty-four year: Bhattacharyya T, Yeon H, Harris MB.   The medical-legal aspects of informed consent in orthopaedic surgery. *J Bone Joint Surg.* 2005;87:2395-2400.

90   "Some people think that doctors and nurses can put scrambled eggs back into the shell." Dorothy Canfield Fischer.

92   When faced with a medical malpractice: Baker T. *The medical malpractice myth.*   Chicago: University of Chicago Press. 2005;108.

94   Real World Numbers: *HealthGrades,* 2004.

96   In general, most apologies: Lazare A.   Apology in medical practice: An emerging clinical skill. *JAMA.* 2006;296:1402.

102   Nearly one out of every: Wachter RM, Shojania KG. *Internal bleeding: The truth behind America's terrifying*

epidemic of medical mistakes. New York: Rugged Land, LLC. 2004;103.

105   a recent review published: Thornburgh N. Teaching doctors to care. *Time.* May 29, 2006;58-59.

106   A 2006 study published: Thornburgh N. Teaching doctors to care. *Time.* May 29, 2006;58-59.

106   A study conducted at Brigham and Women's: Peterson LA, Brennan TA, O'Neil AC. Does housestaff discontinuity of care increase the risk of preventable adverse events? *Ann Intern Med.* 1994;121:866-872.

107   Real World Numbers: Gandhi TK, Kachalia A, Thomas EJ, Puopolo AL, Yoon C, Brennan TA, Studdert DM. Missed and delayed diagnosis in the ambulatory setting: A study of closed malpractice claims. *Ann Intern Med.* 2006;145;488-496.

110   A study published in 2006: Gandhi TK, Kachalia A, Thomas EJ, Puopolo AL, Yoon C, Brennan TA, Studdert DM. Missed and delayed diagnosis in the ambulatory setting: A study of closed malpractice claims. *Ann Intern Med.* 2006;145;488-496.

111   A study published in the: McGlynn EA, Asch SM, Adams J, Keesey J, Hicks J, DeCristofaro A, Kerr EA. The quality of health care delivered to adults in the United States. *N Engl J Med.* 2003;348:2635-2645.

112   Real World Numbers: Wolfe SM. Bad doctors get a free ride. *NYT.* March 4, 2003;A27.

112   A 2006 *Time* magazine "Notebook" section touted: *Time.* July 31, 2006;20.

114   A study published in the: Pierluissi E, Fischer MA, Campbell AR, Landefeld CS. Discussion of medical errors in morbidity and mortality conferences. *JAMA.* 2003;290:2838-2842.

Appendix A
Your State's Malpractice Laws

In nothing do men more nearly approach the gods than in giving health to men.
—Cicero

Every state and jurisdiction has its own laws—criminal and civil—including medical malpractice laws. The ultimate resource regarding medical malpractice laws in your state will always be a defense attorney licensed to practice in your state; however, if you have questions or would like additional information about your state's malpractice laws, a supplement regarding the medical malpractice laws for each state is available. [The author co-wrote each state supplement, along with an experienced medical malpractice defense attorney licensed in that state.]

Each state supplement explains the malpractice laws of that state, providing you a concise yet thorough overview of what you need to know (including the statute of limitations, legal requirements for initiating a claim, caps on damages, medical apology, comparative fault standards, insurance policy consent provision stipulations, expert witness requirements, arbitration, legal standards, representative cases and more). If you would like to know more about your state's medical malpractice laws, supplements for each state are available from Physicians MedicaLegal Prevention, LLC, P.O. Box 9210, Orange Park, Florida 32006, office number (904) 215-7875, fax number (904) 215-7876, or please view the website at www.PhysiciansMedicaLegalPrevention.com.

Appendix B
Practice Areas and Specialties

Is it not also true that no physician . . . considers or enjoins what is for the physician's interest, but that all seek the good of the patient? For we have agreed that a physician . . . is a ruler of bodies, and not a maker of money, have we not?

—Plato

What is sound medical-legal advice offered to a neurologist regarding how to approach a particular patient or complaint may in fact result in a malpractice claim when that same advice is followed by a pediatrician. Different practice areas and physician specialties engender different suggestions, recommendations and advice from the medical-legal perspective.

If you have questions or concerns regarding malpractice issues specific to your particular practice area or specialty, a risk manager, malpractice insurer, medical superior or defense attorney may be able to assist you. However, supplemental material that details specific malpractice issues for different physician specialties and practice areas, as well as for nursing and dentistry, are available from Physicians MedicaLegal Prevention, LLC, P.O. Box 9210, Orange Park, Florida 32006, office number (904)

215-7875, fax number (904) 215-7876, or view the company website at www.PhysiciansMedicaLegalPrevention.com.

Appendix C
The Medical Apology

Science without conscience is but the death of the soul.
—Montaigne

As noted previously, not all states protect a medical apology from being used as evidence of malpractice against a health care provider in a subsequent malpractice lawsuit, and the ones that do may prescribe stipulations and restrictions. A risk manager, malpractice insurer or defense attorney within your state should know your state's laws regarding a medical apology, but if you would like supplemental material on the medial apology within your state please see Appendix A (state supplements).

If you have the opportunity to attend a seminar or lecture regarding the medical apology in your state, it is recommended you do so (even if you do not believe in the effectiveness of medical apologies or know you will never offer one, it is prudent to learn your state's laws regarding admissions against interest). If you are interested in scheduling a medical apology seminar, lecture or conference, Physicians MedicaLegal Prevention can assist you. They can be reached at Physicians MedicaLegal Prevention, LLC, P.O. Box 9210 Orange Park, Florida 32006, office number (904) 215-7875, fax number (904) 215-7876, www.PhysiciansMedicaLegalPrevention.com.

APPENDIX D
Medical Malpractice Defense Attorneys, Listed By State

Wherever law ends, tyranny begins.
—John Locke

The attorneys listed in this appendix all have years of experience successfully representing health care providers in the defense of medical malpractice actions. Your medical malpractice insurer—or the hospital, health care system, medical facility or health care office in which you work—most likely has defense attorneys available to assist you, but if for any reason you want or need your own defense attorney, or if you simply have a legal question, the attorneys listed below may be able to help you. Any attorney listed for your state is qualified to assist you with any questions you might have, and may also be available to represent you in defense of a medical malpractice action, if needed. If, for some reason, the attorney cannot represent you, he will assist you in locating another defense attorney within your state who can.

[Each attorney has voluntarily given permission to have his name listed in Appendix D, without remuneration, obligation or payment or any kind.]

ALABAMA

Thomas Albritton
Albritton, Clifton, Alverson
109 Opp Avenue
Andalusia, AL 36420
tba@albrittons.com
(334) 222-3177

Walter Bates
Starnes & Atchison
100 Brookwood Place
Birmingham, AL 35209
bbates@starneslaw.com
(205) 868-6059

Daniel F. Beasley
Lanier, Ford, Shaver & Payne
200 West Side Square
Huntsville, AL 35801
dfb@lfsp.com
(256) 535-1100

ALASKA

Keith E. Brown
Brown, Waller & Gibbs
821 North Street
Anchorage, AK 99501
brownwag@alaska.net
(907) 276-2050

Robert J. Dickson
Atkinson, Conway & Gagnon
420 "L" Street
Anchorage AK 99501
rjd@acglaw.com
(907) 276-1700

ARIZONA

Roger Morris
Quarles & Brady
2 N. Central Avenue
Phoenix, AZ 85004
rmorris@quarles.com
(602) 229-5269

Anne M. Fulton-Cavett
Cavett & Fulton
6035 E. Grant Road
Tucson, AZ 85712
afulton@dakotacom.net
(520) 733-0100

Kathleen M. Rogers
Slutes, Sakrison & Hill
33 N. Stone Avenue
Tucson, AZ 85701
krogers@sluteslaw.com
(520) 624-6691

Michael J. Ryan
Broening, Oberg, Woods
1122 E. Jefferson Street
Phoenix, AZ 85034
mjr@bowwlaw.com
(602) 271-7700

ARKANSAS

Niki Cung
Kutak Rock
214 West Dickson Street
Fayetteville, AR 72701
niki.cung@kutakrock.com
(479) 973-4200

Wayne Harris
Warner, Smith & Harris
400 Rogers Avenue
Fort Smith, AR 72901
wharris@warnersmith.com
(479) 782-6041

Paul McNeill
Womack, Landis, Phelps
301 W. Washington
Jonesboro, AR 72403
pmcneill@wlpmm-firm.com
(870) 932-0900

CALIFORNIA

Barbara Ann Caulfied
Gordon & Rees
275 Battery Street
San Francisco, CA 94111
bcaulfield@gordonrees.com
(415) 986-5900

Sean D. Cowdrey
Beach Whitman
760 Paseo Camarillo
Camarillo, CA 93010
sean@beachwhitman.com
(805) 388-3100

Randolph M. Even
Randolph M. Even & Associates
5550 Topanga Canyon Blvd.
Woodland Hills, CA 91367
rme@rme-law.com
(818) 226-5444

Sharon L. Hightower
Erickson, Arbuthnot, Kilduff
152 North 3rd Street
San Jose, CA 95112
shightower@eakdl.com
(408) 286-0880

Robert William Hodges
McNamara, Dodge, Ney
1211 Newell Avenue
Walnut Creek, CA 94596
robert.hodges@mcnamaralaw.com
(925) 939-5330

Jimmie Williams
Burnham & Brown
1901 Harrison Street
Oakland, CA 94612
jwilliams@burnhambrown.com
(510) 444-6800

William A. Miller
Higgs, Fletcher & Mack
401 West "A" Street
San Diego, CA 92101
wmiller@higgslaw.com
(619) 236-1551

Chester A. Rogaski, Jr.
Dunn, Rogaski, Preovolos
241 Georgia Street
Vallejo, CA 94590
crogaski@drpwlaw.com
(707) 553-1555

COLORADO

Miles M. Dewhirst
Dewhirst & Dolven
102 South Tejon Street
Colorado Springs, CO 80903
mdewhirst@dewhirstdolven.com
(719) 520-1421

Douglas E. Best
Dickinson, Prud'Homme
730 17th Street
Denver, CO 80202
dbest@dpai-legal.com
(303) 571-4428

Daniel R. McCune
Kennedy, Childs & Fogg
1050 17th Street
Denver, CO 80265
dmccune@kennedy-christopher.com
(303) 825-2700

CONNECTICUT

June M. Sullivan
Halloran & Sage
One Goodwin Square
Hartford, CT 06103
sullivan@halloran-sage.com
(860) 241-4077

Anthony J. Iaconis
Diserio, Martin, O'Connor
One Atlantic Street
Stamford, CT 06901
aiaconis@dmoc.com
(203) 358-0800

Michael P. DelSole
DelSole & DelSole
46 South Whittlesey Ave.
Wallingford, CT 06492
michael@delsoledelsole.com
(203) 284-8000

DELAWARE

Daniel A. Griffith
Marshall, Dennehey, Warner
1220 North Market Street
Wilmington, DE 19899
dagriffith@mdwcg.com
(302) 552-4300

WASHINGTON, D.C.

David Florin
Crowell & Moring
1001 Pennsylvania Ave. NW
Washington, D.C. 20004
dflorin@crowell.com
(202) 624-2755

David Charles Numrych
Bonner, Kiernan, Trebach
1233 20th Street NW
Washington, D.C. 20036
dnumrych@bktc.net
(202) 712-7041

FLORIDA

James DeChurch/Michael Drahos
Fowler, White, Burnett
Offices in Miami, Ft. Lauderdale
West Palm Beach, St. Petersburg
jdechurch@fowler-white.com
(305) 789-9261

Clinton S. Payne
Demahy, Labrador, Drake
2333 Ponce DeLeon Blvd.
Coral Gables, FL 33134
cpayne@dldlawyers.com
(305) 443-4850

Dennis Larry/Jason Peterson
Clark, Partington, Hart, Larry
125 West Romana Street
Pensacola, FL 32501
dlarry@cphlaw.com
(850) 434-9200

Dominic C. MacKenzie
Holland & Knight
50 N. Laura Street
Jacksonville, FL 322202
donny.mackenzie@hklaw.com
(904) 798-7303

GEORGIA

Jason E. Bring
Arnall, Golden, Gregory
171 17th Street NW
Atlanta, GA 30363
jason.bring@agg.com
(404) 873-8162

Joseph P. Durham, Jr.
Langley & Lee
1604 W. Third Avenue
Albany, GA 31707
jdurham@langleyandlee.com
(229) 431-3036

Stephen B. Mosley
Brinson, Askew, Berry
615 West First Street
Rome, GA 30162
smoseley@brinson-askew.com
(706) 291-8853

Douglas W. Smith
Carlock, Copeland, Semler
285 Peachtree Center
Atlanta, GA 30303
dsmith@carlockcopeland.com
(404) 522-8220

HAWAII

William S. Hunt
Alston, Hunt, Floyd & Ang
1001 Bishop Street
Honolulu, HI 96813
whunt@ahfi.com
(808) 524-1800

IDAHO

Theodore O. Creason
Creason, Moore & Dokken
1219 Idaho Street
Lewiston, ID 83501
tcreason@cmd-law.com
(208) 743-1516

David R. Lombardi
Givens Pursley
277 North 6th Street
Boise, ID 83701
drl@givenspursley.com
(208) 388-1200

ILLINOIS

Michelle Adams
Adams Swatek
1250 Executive Place
Geneva, IL 60134
mla@adamsswatek.com
(630) 232-6440

Peter W. Brandt
Livingston, Barger, Brandt
115 West Jefferson
Bloomington, IL 61701
pbrandt@lbbs.com
(309) 828-5281

William J. Brinkmann
Thomas, Mamer & Haughey
30 Main Street
Champaign, IL 61820
wjbrinkmann@tmh-law.com
(217) 351-1500

Robert J. Noe
Bozeman, Neighbour
1630 5th Avenue
Moline, IL 61266
rnoe@bnpn.com
(309) 797-0850

David P. Faulkner
Faulkner & Jensen
6832 Salter Drive
Rockford, IL 61108
dfaulkner@faulknerjensen.com
(815) 963-8050

INDIANA

Mark W. Baeverstad
Rothberg, Logan & Warsco
2100 National City Center
Fort Wayne, IN 46859
mbaeverstad@rlwlawfirm.com
(260) 422-9454

Jon F. Schmoll
Spangler, Jennings
8396 Mississippi Street
Merrillville, IN 46410
jschmoll@sjdlaw.com
(219) 769-2323

Edna M. Koch
Zeigler, Cohen & Koch
9465 Counselors Row
Indianapolis, IN 46240
ekoch@zcklaw.com
(317) 844-5200

David M. McTigue
Herendeen, Kowals, McTigue
419 West Jefferson
South Bend, IN 46601
dbldmr@aol.com
(574) 234-6061

IOWA

Charles Patterson/John Gray
Heidman, Redmond, Fredregill
701 Pierce Street
Sioux City, IA 51101
tom.patterson@heidmanlaw.com
(712) 255-8838

Ralph W. Heninger
Heninger & Heninger
101 West 2nd Street
Davenport, IA 52801
rwh@heningerlaw.com
(563) 324-0418

KANSAS

Eldon L. Boisseau
Law Offices of Eldon L. Boisseau
727 North Waco
Wichita, KS 67203
eldon@boisseau.com
(316) 613-2800

Ted J. McDonald
McCormick, Adam & McDonald
9300 West 110th Street
Overland Park, KS 66210
tmcdonald@mam-firm.com
(913) 647-0670

KENTUCKY

Bradford L. Breeding
Kelley, Brown, Williams
502 West Fifth Street
London, KY 40743
blbreeding@kbwblaw.com
(606) 878-7640

Loretta G. LeBar
Stoll, Keenon, Ogden
300 West Vine Street
Lexington, KY 40507
loretta.lebar@skofirm.com
(502) 419-2571

Pamela W. Popp
Greenebaum, Doll, McDonald
50 East River Center Blvd.
Covington, KY 41011
pwp@gdm.com
(859) 655-6871

David C. Stratton
Stratton, Hogg & Maddox
111 Pike Street
Pikeville, KY 41502
dcstratton@setel.com
(606) 437-7800

James A. Sigler
Whitlow, Roberts, Houston
300 Broadway
Paducah, KY 42002
jsigler@whitlow-law.com
(270) 443-4516

Allison Olczak Wildman
Thompson, Miller, Simpson
600 West Main Street
Louisville, KY 40202
awildman@tmslawplc.com
(502) 585-9900

LOUISIANA

Charles J. Boudreaux, Jr.
Onebane Law Firm
1200 Camellia Blvd.
Lafayette, LA 70508
cjb@onebane.com
(337) 237-2660

Edward Paige Sensenbrenner
Adams & Reese
4500 One Shell Square
New Orleans, LA 70139
paige.sensenbrenner@arlaw.com
(504) 585-0420

Patricia A. Traina
Berrigan, Litchfield, Schonekas
201 St. Charles Avenue
New Orleans, LA 70170
traina@berriganlaw.net
(504) 568-0541

Karen C. Duncan (J.D., R.N.)
Frilot, Partridge
1100 Poydras Street
New Orleans, LA 70163
kduncan@frilotpartridge.com
(504) 599-8026

Marc W. Judice
Judice & Adley
926 Coolidge Blvd.
Lafayette, LA 70503
mwj@judice-adley.com
(337) 235-2405

Virginia Y. Trainor
Phelps Dunbar
445 North Boulevard
Baton Rouge, LA 70802
trainorg@phelps.com
(225) 346-0285

MAINE

Philip M. Coffin, III
Lambert & Coffin
477 Congress Street
Portland, ME 04112
pcoffin@lambertcoffin.com
(207) 874-4000

Elizabeth Germani
Germani & Riggle
93 Exchange Place
Portland, ME 04101
egermani@gr-law.com
(207) 773-7455

MARYLAND

Joseph B. Chazen
Meyers, Rodbell, Rosenbaum
6801 Kenilworth Avenue
Riverdale, MD 20737
jchazen@mrrlaw.net
(301) 699-5800

Jerald J. Oppel
Ober, Kaler, Grimes
120 E. Baltimore Street
Baltimore, MD 21202
jjoppel@ober.com
(410) 347-7338

Charles Martinez
Eccleston & Wolf
729 E. Pratt Street
Baltimore, MD 21202
martinez@ewmd.com
(410) 752-7474

MASSACHUSETTS

Martin C. Foster
Foster & Eldridge
1 Canal Park
Cambridge, MA 02141
mfoster@fosteld.com
(617) 252-3366

Edward T. Hinchey
Sloane & Walsh
3 Center Plaza
Boston, MA 02108
ehinchey@sloanewalsh.com
(617) 523-6010

Peter C. Knight
Morrison Mahoney
250 Summer Street
Boston, MA 02210
pknight@morrisonmahoney.com
(617) 439-7514

MICHIGAN

Daniel G. Beyer
Kerr, Russell & Webster
500 Woodward Avenue
Detroit, MI 48226
dgb@krwlaw.com
(313) 961-0200

Jose T. Brown
Cline, Cline & Griffin
503 S. Saginaw Street
Flint, MI 48502
jbrown@ccglawyers.com
(810) 232-3141

Kimberly A. Berger
Miller, Canfield, Paddock
150 West Jefferson
Detroit, MI 48226
berger@millercanfield.com
(313) 963-6420

William A. Tanoury
Tanoury, Corbert, Shaw
645 Griswold Street
Detroit, MI 48226
william.tanoury@tcsnlaw.com
(313) 964-6300

MINNESOTA

Bradley J. Betlach
Halleland, Lewis, Nilan
220 South 6th Street
Minneapolis, MN 55402
bbetlach@halleland.com
(612) 338-1838

Marlene S. Garvis
Jardine, Logan & O'Brien
8519 Eagle Point Blvd.
Lake Elmo, MN 55042
mgarvis@jlolaw.com
(651) 290-6569

Paul C. Peterson
Lind, Jensen, Sullivan & Peterson
150 South Fifth Street
Minneapolis, MN 55402
paul.peterson@lindjensen.com
(612) 333-3637

MISSISSIPPI

Scott W. Pedigo
Baker, Donelson, Bearman
4268 I-55 North
Jackson, MS 39211
spedigo@bakerdonelson.com
(601) 351-2492

Stephen G. Peresich
Page, Mannino, Peresich
759 Vieux Marche Mall
Biloxi, MS 39533
stephen.peresich@pmp.org
(228) 374-2100

George Q. Evans
Wise, Carter, Child
401 E. Capital Street
Jackson, MS 39205
gqe@wisecarter.com
(601) 968-5572

MISSOURI

Mariam Decker
Oliver, Walker, Wilson
401 Locust Street
Columbia, MO 65205
mdecker@owwlaw.com
(573) 443-3134

Marc K. Erickson
Wagstaff & Cartmell
4740 Grand Avenue
Kansas City, MO 64112
merickson@wcllp.com
(816) 701-1116

Steven Wald
Lathrop & Gage
10 South Broadway
St. Louis, MO 63102
swald@lathropgage.com
(314) 613-2542

Philip Willman/Angela Pozzo
Moser & Marsalek
200 North Broadway
St. Louis, MO 63102
apozzo@moser.com
(314) 421-5364

MONTANA

Lawrence F. Daly
Garlington, Lohn & Robinson
199 West Pine Street
Missoula, MT 59807
lfdaly@garlington.com
(406) 523-2549

Jacqueline Lenmark
Keller, Reynolds, Drake
50 S. Last Chance Gulch
Helena, MT 59601
jtlenmark@kellerlawmt.com
(406) 442-0230

NEBRASKA

Patrick G. Vipond
Lamson, Dugan & Murray
10306 Regency Parkway Drive
Omaha, NE 68114
pgv@ldmlaw.com
(402) 397-7300

NEVADA

David J. Mortensen
Alverson, Taylor, Mortensen
7401 West Charleston Blvd.
Las Vegas, NV 89117
dmortensen@alversontaylor.com
(702) 384-7000

Melissa Exline
Perry & Spann
6130 Plumas Street
Reno, NV 89509
mexline@perryspann.com
(775) 829-2002

NEW HAMPSHIRE

Ronald L. Snow
Orr & Reno
One Eagle Square
Concord, NH 03302
rlsnow@orr-reno.com
(603) 224-2381

Michael P. Lehman
Sulloway & Hollis
9 Capitol St./29 School St.
Concord, NH 03301
mlehman@sulloway.com
(603) 224-2341

NEW JERSEY

Phillip J. Duffy
Gibbons, Del Deo, Dolan
One Riverfront Plaza
Newark, NJ 07102
pjduffy@gibbonslaw.com
(973) 596-4821

Patrick J. Dwyer
Smith, Stratton, Wise
2 Research Way
Princeton, NJ 08540
pdwyer@smithstratton.com
(609) 924-6000

Charles F. Harris
Mason, Griffin & Pierson
101 Poor Farm Road
Princeton, NJ 08540
c.harris@mgplaw.com
(609) 436-1206

Gilbert S. Leeds
Schenck, Price, Smith
10 Washington Street
Morristown, NJ 07963
gsl@spsk.com
(973) 539-1000

Douglas V. Sanchez
Cruiser, Mitchell & Sanchez
401 Hackensack Avenue
Hackensack, NJ 07601
dsanchez@cmlawfirm.com
(201) 543-5808

NEW MEXICO

Mary M. Behm
Keleher & McLeod
201 3rd Street NW
Albuquerque, NM 87103
mb@keleher-law.com
(505) 346-9130

Edward W. Shepherd
Hatch, Allen & Shepherd
4801 Lang Avenue NW
Albuquerque, NM 87199
nshperherd@hatchlaw.com
(505) 341-0110

NEW YORK

Robert Gibson
Heidell, Pittoni, Murphy
99 Park Avenue
New York, NY 10016
rgibson@hpmb.com
(212) 286-8585

Thomas M. Prato
Brown & Tarantino
45 Exchange Boulevard
Rochester, NY 14614
tprato@btattys.com
(585) 454-3377

Victor Alan Oliveri
Gibson, McAskill, Crosby
69 Delaware Ave.
Buffalo, NY 14202
voliveri@gmclaw.com
(716) 856-4200

Lauren Melissa Snyder
Thuillez, Ford, Gold
20 Corporate Woods Blvd.
Albany, NY 12211
lsnyder@tfgjlaw.com
(518) 455-9952

Andrew S. Kaufman
Kaufman, Borgeest, Ryan
99 Park Avenue
New York, NY 10016
akaufman@kbrny.com
(212) 980-9600

Abe M. Rychik
Melito & Adolfsen
233 Broadway
New York, NY 10279
amr@melitoadolfsen.com
(212) 238-8940

NORTH CAROLINA

Richard V. Bennett
Bennett & Guthrie
1560 Westbrook Plaza Drive
Winston-Salem, NC 27103
rbennett@bennett-guthrie.com
(336) 765-3121

William P. Daniel
Young, Moore
3101 Glenwood Avenue
Raleigh, NC 27612
wpd@youngmoorelaw.com
(919) 782-6860

Barry S. Cobb
Yates, McLamb & Weyher
421 Fayetteville Street
Raleigh, NC 27601
bcobb@ymwlaw.com
(919) 835-0900

Thomas E. Harris
Harris, Creech, Ward
325 Pollock Street
New Bern, NC 28563
the@hcwb.net
(252) 638-6666

Harriett T. Smalls
Smith Moore
300 N. Greene Street
Greensboro, NC 27401
harriett.smalls@smithmoorelaw.com
(336) 378-5424

NORTH DAKOTA

Scott D. Jensen
Camrud, Maddock, Olson
401 DeMers Avenue
Grand Forks, ND 58201
sjensen@camrudlaw.com
(701) 775-5595

OHIO

Julie Callsen
Tucker, Ellis & West
1150 Huntington Building
Cleveland, OH 44115
julie.callsen@tuckerellis.com
(216) 696-2286

Susan Blasik-Miller
Freund, Freeze & Arnold
One South Main Street
Dayton, OH 45402
sblasikm@ffalaw.com
(937) 222-2424

James F. Nooney
Eastman & Smith
One Seagate
Toledo, OH 43604
jfnooney@eastmansmith.com
(419) 247-1692

Mark L. Schumacher
Freund, Freeze & Arnold
65 East State Street
Columbus, OH 43215
mschumac@ffalaw.com
(614) 827-7300

Deborah R. Lydon
Dinsmore & Shohl
255 East 5th Street
Cincinnati, OH 45202
lydon@dinslaw.com
(513) 977-8344

OKLAHOMA

Margaret M. Clarke
Rhodes, Hiernoymous, Jones
100 West 5th Street
Tulsa, OK 74103
mclarke@rhodesokla.com
(918) 582-1173

Alexander C. Vosler
Johnson & Hanan
100 N. Broadway
Oklahoma City, OK 73102
avosler@johnsonhanan.com
(405) 232-6100

OREGON

Thomas F. Armosino
Frohnmayer, Deatherage, Pratt
2592 East Barnett Road
Medford, OR 97504
deatherage@fdfirm.com
(541) 779-2333

Connie Elkins McKelvey
Hoffman, Hart & Wagner
1000 SW Broadway
Portland, OR 97205
cem@hhw.com
(503) 222-4499

PENNSYLVANIA

James J. Dodd-o
Thomas, Thomas & Hafer
3400 Bath Pike
Bethlehem, PA 18017
jdoddo@tthlaw.com
(610) 332-7000

Richard A. Kolb
White & Williams
1800 One Liberty Place
Philadelphia, PA 19103
kolbr@whiteandwilliams.com
(215) 864-7112

Christopher W. Mattson
Barley, Snyder, Senft
126 E. King Street
Lancaster, PA 17602
cmattson@barley.com
(717) 299-5201

Joseph J. McHale
Stradley, Ronon, Stevens
30 Valley Stream Parkway
Malvern, PA 19355
jmchale@stradley.com
(610) 640-5800

James R. Miller
Dickie, McCamey & Chilcote
Two PPG Place
Pittsburgh, PA 15222
millerj@dmclaw.com
(412) 392-5238

Paul K. Vey
Pietragallo, Bosick, Gordon
301 Grant Street
Pittsburgh, PA 15219
pkv@pbandg.com
(412) 263-2000

RHODE ISLAND

R. Kelly Sheridan
Roberts, Carroll, Feldstein
Ten Weybosset Street
Providence, RI 02903
ksheridan@rcfp.com
(401) 521-7000

SOUTH CAROLINA

Kay Gaffney Crowe
Barnes, Alford, Stork
1613 Main Street
Columbia, SC 29202
kay@basjlaw.com
(803) 799-1111

G. Dewey Oxner, Jr.
Haynsworth, Sinkler, Boyd
75 Beattie Place
Greenville, SC 29601
gdoxner@hsblawfirm.com
(864) 240-3208

SOUTH DAKOTA

Craig A. Kennedy
Kennedy, Rokahr, Pier
322 Walnut Street
Yankton, SD 57078
ckennedy@yanktonlawyers.com
(605) 665-3000

Lonnie R. Braun
Thomas, Nooney, Braun
1301 Omaha Street
Rapid City, SD 57701
lrbraun@mtnlaw.com
(605) 348-7516

TENNESSEE

Steven E. Anderson
Walker, Bryant, Tipps
2300 One Nashville Place
Nashville, TN 37219
sanderson@walkerbryant.com
(615) 313-6000

Nicholas E. Bragorgos
McNabb, Bragorgos
81 Monroe Avenue
Memphis, TN 38103
nbragorgos@mbb-law.com
(901) 624-0640

David M. Cook
The Hardison Law Firm
119 South Main Street
Memphis, TN 38103
dcook@thehardisonlawfirm.com
(901) 525-8776

Sharel V. Hooper
Spears, Moore, Rebman
801 Broad Street
Chattanooga, TN 37401
svh@smrw.com
(423) 756-7000

Wayne A. Kline
Hodges, Doughty & Carson
617 Main Street
Knoxville, TN 37901
wkline@hdclaw.com
(865) 292-2307

Robert E. Parker
Parker, Lawrence, Cantrell
200 Fourth Avenue North
Nashville, TN 37214
rparker@plcd.com
(615) 255-7500

TEXAS

William A. Abernathy
Donnell, Abernathy
555 North Carancahua
Corpus Christi, TX 78478
babernathy@dakpc.com
(361) 888-5551

Dan Ballard
Ballard & Simmons
701 Brazos Street
Austin, TX 78701
dan9705706@yahoo.com
(512) 703-5021

Mark T. Beaman
Germer, Gertz
301 Congress Avenue
Austin, TX 78701
mbeaman@germer-austin.com
(512) 472-0288

D. Faye Caldwell
Caldwell & Clinton
1001 Fannin
Houston, TX 77002
fcaldwell@caldwellclinton.com
(713) 654-3000

Curry L. Cooksey
Orgain, Bell & Tucker
10077 Grogans Mill Road
The Woodlands, TX 77380
clc@obt.com
(713) 572-8772

Charles A. Deacon
Fulbright & Jaworski
300 Convent Street
San Antonio, TX 78205
cdeacon@fulbright.com
(210) 224-5575

Caroline C. Harrison
Cantley & Hanger
801 Cherry Street
Fort Worth, TX 76102
charrison@canteyhanger.com
(817) 877-2827

Max E. Wright
Wright & Jackson
505 N. Big Spring Street
Midland, TX 79701
mwright@wrightlawfirmpc.com
(432) 686-0080

D. Bowen Berry
Berry & Randall
1701 Market Street
Dallas, TX 75202
berry@berryrandall.com
(214) 915-9800

James D. Bertsch
Touchstone, Bernays
1201 Elm Street
Dallas, TX 75270
james.bertsch@tbjbs.com
(214) 741-1166

Benjamin H. Davidson
McCleskey, Harriger
5010 University
Lubbock, TX 79413
bdavidson@mhbg.com
(806) 796-7306

Slater C. Elza
Underwood, Wilson, Berry
500 S. Taylor Street
Amarillo, TX 79105
slater.elza@uwlaw.com
(806) 379-0347

Alan D. Harrel
Atchley, Russell, Waldrop
1710 Moores Lane
Texarkana, TX 75503
aharrel@arwhlaw.com
(903) 792-8246

H. Keith Myers
Mounce, Green, Myers
100 N. Stanton Street
El Paso, TX 79901
myers@mgmsg.com
(915) 532-2000

Christopher D. DeMeo
Sheehey, Serpe & Ware
909 Fannin
Houston, TX 77010
cdemeo@sswpc.com
(713) 951-1089

UTAH

Charles W. Dahlquist, II
Kirton & McConkie
60 East South Temple
Salt Lake City, UT 84111
cdahlquist@kmclaw.com
(801) 321-4807

Robert G. Wright
Richards, Brandt, Miller
50 South Main Street
Salt Lake City, UT 84144
robert-wright@rbmn.com
(801) 531-2000

Michael J. Miller
Strong & Hanni
3 Triad Center
Salt Lake City, UT 84180
mmiller@strongandhanni.com
(801) 532-7080

VERMONT

Ritchie E. Berger
Dinse, Knapp & McAndrew
209 Battery Street
Burlington, VT 05402
rberger@dinse.com
(802) 864-5751

VIRGINIA

James Fitzpatrick (J.D., M.D.)
LeClair & Ryan
225 Reinekers Lane
Alexandria, VA 22314
james.fitzpatrick@leclairryan.com
(703) 647-5931

Tracey Cover (J.D., C.R.N.A.)
McCarthy, Massey, Mitchell
9200 Church Street
Manassas, VA 20110
tcover@mmmlegal.com
(703) 330-2726

Charles Y. Sipe
Goodman, Allen, Filetti
1020 Ednam Center
Charlottesville, VA 22903
csipe@goodmanallen.com
(434) 817-2180

Susan M. Waddell
Guynn, Memmer & Dillon
415 South College Avenue
Salem, VA 24153
susan.waddell@g-mpc.com
(540) 387-2320

Carlyle R. "Randy" Wimbish, III
Sands, Anderson, Marks & Miller
801 East Main Street
Richmond, VA 23219
rwimbish@sanderson.com
(804) 783-7257

Keith T. Shiner
Reed Smith
3110 Fairview Park Drive
Falls Church, VA 22042
kshiner@reedsmith.com
(703) 641-4221

WASHINGTON

Gregory B. Curwen
Gierke, Curwen, Metzler
2102 North Pearl Street
Tacoma, WA 98406
gcurwen@gcmelaw.com
(253) 752-1600

Dennis L. Fluegge
Meyer, Fluegge, Tenney
230 South Second Street
Yakima, WA 98907
fluegge@mftlaw.com
(509) 575-8500

Michael Madden
Bennett, Bigelow, Leedom
1700 7th Street
Seattle, WA 98101
mmadden@bbllaw.com
(206) 622-5511

Mary K. McIntyre
McIntyre & Barnes
1215 Fourth Avenue
Seattle, WA 98161
marym@mcblegal.com
(206) 682-8285

WEST VIRGINIA

Holly S. Planinsic
Herndon, Morton, Herndon
83 Edgington Lane
Wheeling, WV 26003
hplaninsic@hmhy.com
(304) 242-2300

David L. Shuman
Shuman, McCuskey, Slicer
1411 Virginia Street East
Charleston, WV 25339
dshuman@shumanlaw.com
(304) 345-1400

WISCONSIN

Sean M. Gaynor
Leib & Katt
740 N. Plankinton Ave.
Milwaukee, WI 53203
smg@leibkatt.com
(414) 276-8816

WYOMING

Jeffrey C. Brinkerhoff
Brown, Drew, Massey
159 N. Wolcott Street
Casper, WY 82601
jcb@browndrew.com
(307) 234-1000

REFERENCES

Arora V, Johnson J, Lovinger D, Humphrey HJ, Meltzer DO. Communication failures in patient sign-out and suggestions for improvement: A critical incident analysis. *Qual Saf Healthcare.* 2005;14:401-407.

Baker T. *The medical malpractice myth.* Chicago: University of Chicago Press. 2005.

Banja J. Moral courage in medicine—disclosing medical error. *Bioethics Forum.* 2001;17:7-11.

Bates DW, Cullen DJ, Laird N. Incidence of adverse drug events and potential adverse drug events: Implications for prevention: ADE Prevention Group Study. *JAMA.* 1995;274:29-34.

Bernat JL, Peterson LM. Pateint-centered informed consent in surgical practice. *Arch Surg.* 2006;141:86-92.

Bhattacharyya T, Yeon H, Harris MB. The medical-legal aspects of informed consent in orthopaedic surgery. *J Bone Joint Surg.* 2005;87:2395-2400.

Blackstone, Sir William. *Commentaries on the laws of England: 1765-1767.* London: Lawbook Exchange. 3d Rev. Ed. 2004.

Blendon RJ, DesRoches CM, Brodie M, Benson JM, Rosen AB, Schneider E, Altman DE, Zapert K, Herrmann MJ,

Steffson AE. Views of practicing physicians and the public on medical errors. *N Engl J Med*. 2002;346:1933-1940.

Bovbjerg RR, Dubay LC, Kenney GM, Norton SA. Defensive medicine and tort reform: new evidence in an old bottle. *J Health Polit Policy Law*. 1996;21:267-288.

Brennan TA, Sox CM, Burstin HR. Relation between negligent adverse events and the outcomes of medical malpractice litigation. *N Engl J Med*. 1996;335:1963-1967.

Budnitz DS, Pollock DA, Weidenbach KN, Mendelsohn AB, Schroeder TJ, Annest JL. National surveillance of emergency department visits for outpatient adverse drug events. *JAMA*. 2006;296:1858-1866.

Clinton HR, Obama B. Making patient safety the centerpiece of medical liability reform. *N Engl J Med*. 2006;354:2205-2208.

Duclos CW, Eichler M, Taylor L, Quintela J, Main DS, Pace W, Staton EW. Patient perspectives of patient-provider communication after adverse events. *Int'l J Qual Healthcare*. 2005;17:479-486.

Ethics manual: fourth edition: American College of Physicians *Ann Intern Med*. 1998;128:576-594.

Feddock CA, Hoellein AR, Griffith CH, Wilson JF, Becker NS, Bowerman JL, Caudill TS. Are continuity clinic patients less satisfied when residents have a heavy inpatient workload? *Eval Health Prof*. 2005;28:390-399.

Forster HP, Schwartz J, DeRenzo E. Reducing legal risk by practicing patient-centered medicine. *Arch Intern Med*. 2002;162:1217-1219.

Friedenberg RM. Malpractice reform. *Radiology*. 2004;231:3-6.

Friedenberg RM. Patient-doctor relationships. *Radiology*. 2003;226:306-308.

Gallagher TH, Waterman AD, Ebers AG, Fraser VJ, Levinson W. Patients' and physicians' attitudes regarding the disclosure of medical errors. *JAMA*. 2003;289:1001-1007.

Gandhi TK, Kachalia A, Thomas EJ, Puopolo AL, Yoon C, Brennan TA, Studdert DM. Missed and delayed diagnosis in the ambulatory setting: A study of closed malpractice claims. *Ann Intern Med*. 2006;145;488-496.

Gawande AA, Studdert DM, Orav EJ, Brennan TA, Zinner MJ. Risk factors for retained instruments and sponges after surgery. *N Engl J Med*. 2003;348:229-235.

Gibbs N, Bower A. What scares doctors: What insiders know about our health-care system that the rest of us need to learn. *Time*. May 1, 2006:42-52.

Gibson RB, Del Vecchio LA. Effects of 'full disclosure' on litigation. *For The Defense*. November 2006:41-47.

Harvard Medical Practice Study. *Patients, doctors, and lawyers: Medical injury, malpractice litigation, and patient compensation in New York: The report of the Harvard Medical Practice Study to the State of New York*. Cambridge: Harvard University. 1990.

Hickson GB, Clayton EW, Githens PB, Sloan FA. Factors that prompted families to file medical malpractice claims following perinatal injuries. *JAMA*. 1992;267:1359-1363.

Hickson GB, Federspiel CF, Pichert JW, Miller CS, Gauld-Jaeger J, Bost P. Patient complaints and malpractice risk. *JAMA*. 2002;287:2951-2957.

Hobgood C, Weiner B, Tamayo-Sarver JH. Medical error identification, disclosure, and reporting: Do emergency medicine provider groups differ? *Acad Emerg Med*. 2006;13:443-451.

Holder AR. Medical Errors. *Hematology*. 2005;2005:503-506.

Institute of Medicine. Committee on quality of health care in America. *Crossing the Quality Chasm: A New Health System for the 21st Century.* Washington, DC: National Academy Press; 2001.

Jagsi R, Kitch BT, Weinstein DF, Campbell EG, Hutter M, Weissman JS. Residents report on adverse events and their causes. *Arch Intern Med.* 2005;165:2607-2613.

Joint Commission on Accreditation of Healthcare Organizations. *Revisions to Joint Commission Standards in Support of Patient Safety and Medical Healthcare Error Reduction: effective July 1, 2001.* Galveston: University of Texas Medical Branch; 2001.

Kereiakes DJ, Willerson JT. Healthcare on trial: America's medical malpractice crisis. *Circulation.* 2004;109:2939-2941.

Kraman SS, Hamm G. Risk management: Extreme honesty may be the best policy. *Ann Intern Med.* 1999;131:963-967.

Kohn LT, Corrigan J, Donaldson MS. *To Err is Human: Building a Safer Health System.* Washington, DC: National Academy Press; 2000.

Lamb RM, Studdert DM, Bohmer MJ, Berwick DM, Brennan TA. Hospital disclosure practices: Results of a national survey. *Health Aff.* 2003;22:73-83.

Larsen KM, Smith CK. Assessment of non-verbal communication in the patient-physician interview. *Journal of Family Practice. 1981:12;481-488.*

Lazare A. Apology in medical practice: An emerging clinical skill. *JAMA.* 2006;296:1401-1404.

Leape LL. Reporting adverse events. *N Engl J Med.* 2002;347:1633-1638.

References — 159

Levinson W, Roter DL, Mullooly JP, Dull VT, Frankel RM. Physician-patient communication. The relationship with malpractice claims among primary care physicians and surgeons. *JAMA*. 1997;277:553-559.

Localio AR, Lawthers AG, Brennan TA, Laird NM, Hebert LE, Peterson LM, Newhouse JP, Weiler PC, Hiatt HH. Relation between malpractice claims and adverse events due to negligence, results of the Harvard Medical Practice Study III. *N Engl J Med*. 1991;325:245-251.

Lowenstein J. Where have all the giants gone? Reconciling medical education and the traditions of patient care with limitations on resident hours. *Perspect Biol Med*. 2003;46:273-282.

Marvel MK, Epstein RM, Flowers K, Beckham HB. Soliciting the patient agenda: Have we improved? *JAMA. 1999;281:283-287.*

McGlynn EA, Asch SM, Adams J, Keesey J, Hicks J, DeCristofaro A, Kerr EA. The Quality of health care delivered to adults in the United States. *N Engl J Med*. 2003;348:2635-2645.

Mello MM, Brennan TA. Deterrence of medical errors: Theory and evidence for malpractice reform. *Tex Law Rev*. 2002;80:1595-1637.

Mycyk MB, McDaniel MR, Fotis MA, Regalado J. Hospitalwide adverse drug events before and after limiting weekly hours of medical residents to 80. *Am J Health Syst Pharm*. 2005;62:1592-1595.

Orlander JD, Barber TW, Fincke BG. The morbidity and mortality conference: The delicate nature of learning from error. *Acad Med* 2002;77:1001-1006.

Pagano LA, Lookinland S. Nursing morbidity and mortality conferences: Promoting clinical excellence. *Am J Crit Care*. 2006;15:78-85.

Peterson LA, Brennan TA, O'Neil AC. Does housestaff discontinuity of care increase the risk of preventable adverse events? *Ann Intern Med.* 1994;121:866-872.

Philibert I, Leach DC. Re-framing continuity of care for this century. *Qual Saf Healthcare.* 2005;14:394-396.

Pierluissi E, Fischer MA, Campbell AR, Landefeld CS. Discussion of medical errors in morbidity and mortality conferences. *JAMA.* 2003;290:2838-2842.

Roumm AR, Sciamanna CN, Nash DB. Healthcare provider use of private sector internal error-reporting systems. *Am J Med Qual.* 2005;20:304-312.

Runciman WB, Merry AF, Tito F. Error, blame, and the law in health care: An antipodean perspective. *Ann Intern Med.* 2003;138:974-979.

Shoenbaum S, Bovberg RR. Malpractice reform must include steps to prevent medical injury. *Ann Intern Med.* 2004;140:51-53.

Sirio CA, Segel KT, Keyser DJ, Harrison EI, Lloyd JC, Weber RJ, Muto CA, Webster DG, Pisowicz V, Feinstein KW. Pittsburgh regional health care initiative: A systems approach for achieving perfect patient care. *Health Aff.* 2003;22:157-165.

Sorokin R, Riggio JM, Hwang C. Attitudes about patient safety: A survey of physicians-in-training. *Am J Med Qual.* 2005;20:70-77.

Stelfox H, Ghandi T, Orav E, Gustafson M. The relation of patient satisfaction with complaints against physicians and malpractice lawsuits. *Am J Med.* 2005;10:1126-1133.

Studdert DM, Mello MM, Brennan TA. Medical malpractice. *N Engl J Med.* 2004;350:283-292.

Studdert DM, Mello MM, Gawande AA, Gandhi TK, Kachalia A, Yoon C, Puopolo AL, Brennan TA. Claims, errors, and compensation payments in medical malpractice litigation. *N Engl J Med.* 2006;354:2024-2033.

Studdert DM, Mello MM, Sage WM, DesRoches CM, Peugh J, Zapert K, Brennan TA. Defensive medicine among high-risk specialist physicians in a volatile malpractice environment. *JAMA.* 2005;293:2609-2617.

Sutcliffe KM, Lewton E, Rosenthal MM. Communication failures: An insidious contributor to medical mishaps. *Acad Med.* 2004;79:186-194.

Taft L. Apology and medical mistake. Opportunity or foil? *Ann Health Law.* 2005;14:55-94.

Thomas EJ, Studdert DM, Brennan TA. The reliability of medical record review for estimating adverse event rates. *Ann Intern Med.* 2002;136:812-816.

Thomas EJ, Studdert DM, Burstin HR, Orav EJ, Seena T, Williams EJ, Howard KM, Weiler PC, Brennan TA. Incidence and types of adverse events and negligent care in Utah and Colorado. *Med Care.* 2000;38:261-271.

Thornburgh N. Teaching doctors to care. *Time.* May 29, 2006;58-59.

Van Eaton EG, Horvath KD, Lober B, Pellegrini CA. Organizing the transfer of patient care information: The development of a computerized resident sign-out system. *Surgery.* 2004;136:5-13.

van Tilburg CM, Leistikow IP, Rademaker CMA, Bierings MB, van Dijk ATH. Healthcare failure mode and effect analysis: A useful proactive risk analysis in a pediatric oncology ward. *Qual Saf Healthcare.* 2006;15:58-63.

Van Eaton EG, Horvath KD, Pellegrini CA. Professionalism and the shift mentality. *Arch Surg.* 2005;140:230-235.

Volpp K GM, Grande D. Residents' suggestions for reducing errors in teaching hospitals. *N Engl J Med.* 2003;348:851-855.

Wachter RM, Shojania KG. *Internal bleeding: The truth behind America's terrifying epidemic of medical mistakes.* New York: Rugged Land, LLC. 2004.

White MJ. The value of liability in medical malpractice. *Health Aff.* 1994;13:75-87.

Wolfe SM. Bad doctors get a free ride. *NYT.* March 4, 2003;A27.

Zuckerman S. Medical Malpractice: Claims, legal costs, and the practice of defensive medicine. *Health Aff.* 1984;3:128-133.

INDEX

> *Physician, heal thyself.*
> **—Luke 4:23**

Please contact

Physicians MedicaLegal Prevention, LLC

for additional materials and services:

State Supplements
Physician Specialty Supplements
Live Seminar Presentations
Seminar DVDs and Videos
The Medical Apology
Quarterly Newsletter Updates
Books on Tape/Audio Books

www.PhysiciansMedicaLegalPrevention.com

P.O. Box 9210
Orange Park, Florida 32006
(904) 215-7875
(904) 215-7876 fax

Quick Order Form

Fax Orders: 904-215-7876. Send this form.

Telephone Orders: 904-215-7875

Postal Orders: Physicians MedicaLegal Prevention, LLC
                     P.O. Box 9210
                     Orange Park, Florida 32006

Please send _____ copies of *Physician, Protect Thyself* to
Name: _____
Address: _____
City: _____ State: _____ Zip: _____
Telephone: _____
Email address: _____

Payment: ☐ Check   ☐ Credit Card

☐ Visa   ☐ MasterCard   ☐ AMEX   ☐ Discover

Card Number: _____
Name on Card: _____ Exp. Date:_____

Each copy is $24.95, plus $4.95 shipping and handling.

Bulk Order Discount Pricing
10 to 49 . . . . $23.50 each
50 to 99 . . . . $22.50 each
100 to 249 . . . . $21.25 each
250 to 499 . . . . $19.95 each
500 or more . . . . $18.50 each

(additional educational institution discounts available)

www.PhysiciansMedicaLegalPrevention.com